CONTENTS

INTRODUCTION

This is the second book in the series, Thank Goodness They Can't Talk, set in Shropshire, England.

This book contains another collection of true adventures and unbelievable scenarios that Geoff finds himself in as he cares for unpredictable cats and dogs.

Geoff's unique stories are diversified and are not just about cats and dogs. For example, Geoff has a phenomenal experience with an elusive woodland bird that wasn't believed by experts at that time.

Prefixing each chapter is an outstanding caricature that gives a visual clue to the next extraordinary chain of events.

Everyone loves their pets, and their owners take great care in deciding where their cats and dogs will be staying.

But, did they know what their precious pets got up to?

They had absolutely no idea!

For sure, regarding Geoff's crazy adventures, it was a good job the animals couldn't talk!

Following is the hilarious story of Pepper.

SETTING THE SCENE

Please study Home Sweet Home because a lot of the action took place in this area. And when I say action. I mean—ACTION

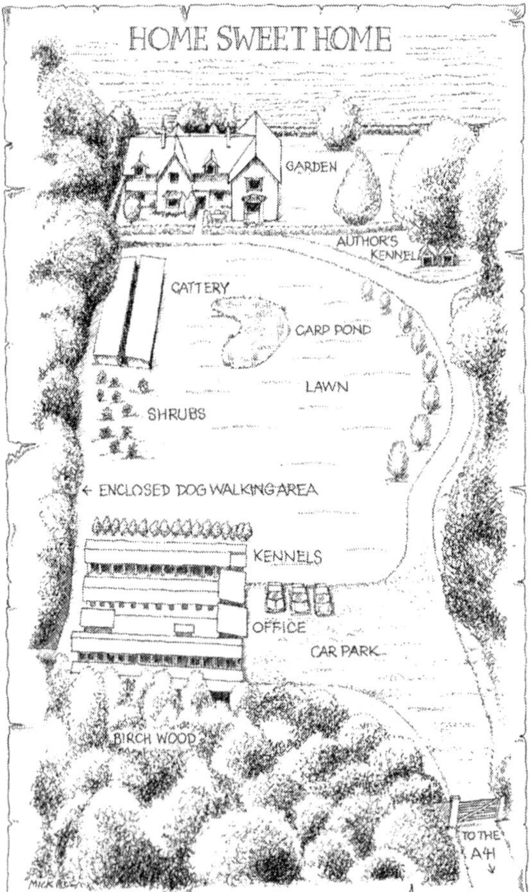

CHAPTER 1

Pepper the Trophy Hunter

Pepper was a male ginger tabby belonging to a couple Mike and Jan. Mike was our solicitor and I met him when he joined the firm of Gwynne & Sons which I had used for several years. Mike and I became friendly and to cut a long story short, Kathy and Jan became very close friends.

Mike was stocky, with short, thick black curly hair, black-rimmed glasses and a short black moustache. (Take note, Mike's thick curly hair is crucial to this story.) Jan was a slim, light blue-eyed, strawberry blonde, with hair neatly cut to her shoulders.

We made friends with Pepper long before he came to stay with us in the cattery because we met him many times at Mike and Jan's house. He was a very placid cat and friendly towards humans, but not so friendly toward the wildlife in the area.

In fact, he caught and ate the beggars!

Pepper could only be described as a very proficient hunter. He liked nothing better than to bring his trophies back, dead or alive, to proudly show his 'mum' and 'dad', (Mike & Jan). Sadly, M & J were far too often finding whole or part-eaten bodies of Pepper's unfortunate victims in various rooms of their house.

Pepper was a very strong cat and one day he even managed to drag a dead full-grown rabbit through the small top-light window to Mike and Jan's upstairs bedroom. Some achievement, believe me. To achieve this remarkable feat, Pepper, with the rabbit clenched firmly in his jaws jumped onto the refuse bin by the back door of their house and then climbed onto the apex roof of the porch. Then he managed to scramble up onto a higher roof that was below Mike and Jan's bedroom window and finally struggled through the small top window that was mistakenly left ajar. I am sure he was very proud when he finally dumped the bloodied body of the dead rabbit, smack-bang in the middle of Mike and Jan's bed.

When they got home from work, they were not too amused to find that particular trophy, or should I say Pepper's present to them, sprawled bloody and lifeless across their bed.

Later, in a conversation around the dinner table, Mike and Jan were shocked when I informed them that rabbits are always, and I mean always infested with hundreds and hundreds of parasitic fleas. They were not too happy when I shared more of my knowledge about nature. It is fleas that help spread the disgusting virus myxomatosis. The news gets worse. Fleas can carry tapeworm larvae, and when a flea bites its host, the unfortunate host is infected with a live tapeworm. Here is more bad news. In humans, tapeworms can grow to more than twelve feet long...

Arghhh!

I endeavoured to explain to Mike and Jan, that to my knowledge, humans are not susceptible to that dreadful disease myxomatosis. I always smile to myself when I remember the look of horror on their faces while I was giving them some of my knowledgeable information. Well, I have to admit, I was winding them up, maybe just a little bit!

At the end of this chapter, there are some very interesting facts about wild rabbits and myxomatosis.

After those alarming facts about fleas and tapeworms, here comes an exciting hilarious story, about a tiny furry trophy of Pepper's which culminates in the crazy climax to this chapter. I can absolutely guarantee it will make you laugh out loud, especially when we get to the part about Mike's hair.

One evening Kathy and I were at Pepper's house, or I should I say Mike and Jan's, enjoying a very nice dinner. The food Jan cooked was always outstanding and was something we always looked forward to.

By the way, it was not a rabbit!

The subjects we covered in our conversations were extremely varied and as the wine slipped down so easily the conversation became light-hearted and as usual, the laughter would start. We had a lovely evening chatting around the dinner table and as it was becoming quite late and bedtime was not too far away, we retired to the lounge for tea and coffee and a small brandy for me because it was Kathy's turn to drive.

But, this particular night turned out to be a little bit more exciting than the norm.

And much later than usual...

Mike was getting the brandy and liquors from a cupboard in the lounge as Kathy and I were relaxing on the sofa and Jan was in the kitchen preparing hot drinks. Suddenly, we heard a terrible shrieking scream from somewhere in the house. Surely it had to be Jan, although it sounded as if the screaming was coming from upstairs.

Kathy looked on in amazement as Jan's two brave heroes (Mike and Geoff) both tried to get through the lounge doorway at the same time, therefore, colliding with each other in the process.

Mike shouted out loudly,

“WHERE ARE YOU JAN?”

She answered with a tremor in her voice,

“I’m here in the kitchen. Pepper has just come in with a mouse. I’m sure it’s still alive. He’s just run up the stairs with it.”

Behind me, out of the corner of my eye, on hearing this startling piece of mouse information, I saw Kathy, in a lightning move kick off her shoes and jump up onto the safety of the lounge sofa.

The only things that Kathy is terrified of in her life are rats and mice. She hadn’t even seen the little mouse in question and she had already put as much distance as possible between her and the floor.

Mike and Geoff, who were Jan's and now Kathy's intrepid heroes, ran up the stairs taking two steps at a time with brave Jan in close pursuit. Jan ran into the main bedroom and her lovely pale blue eyes were wide open with sheer terror as she jumped onto the safety of a chair.

She screamed,

"WHERE'S IT GONE?"

With me being used to wildlife, I decided to take over the reins of the situation.

I said,

"I bet he's gone under the bed where it's dark. I'll close the bedroom door to stop him from getting out."

Jan was horrified and said,

"Oh, no you won't"

"Don't you dare?"

"I don't want that horrible thing loose in here!"

"Leave that door wide open!"

So, I left it open.

BIG, BIG, MISTAKE!

Mike and I knelt down on our hands and knees on either side of the bed, we looked underneath to see if Pepper's lively trophy was there.

And sure enough, he was.

The poor unfortunate mouse was huddled up under the centre of the bed.

I banged hard with the flat of my hand on the shiny wooden floor.

The tiny mouse shot out.

Jan shrieked and pointed,

"THERE IT GOES!"

Pepper, with not a care in the world, was totally oblivious to the ongoing proceedings regarding Jan and Kathy's furry nightmare. He just sat on the landing giving his tummy a good licking with one back leg pointing up at the ceiling.

Kathy, still barefooted, (she can run faster without shoes) bravely ventured upstairs onto the landing to watch the fun and games and stood on a convenient chair.

I rushed out in hot pursuit of the tiny furry rodent with Mike close on my heels, and we were just in time to see the mouse disappear into another bedroom.

I shouted,

“OH NO!”

“Why didn’t we think to shut all the doors?”

“Kathy, get down from there now, and close all the doors.”

She responded,

“NO! I will not!”

I shouted to Jan to ask her to close the doors and, not surprisingly got a similar response with a few more colourful words thrown in as well.

Mike came to the rescue.

“Don’t worry Geoff, I’ll close them. You see if you can find where he’s hiding in that bedroom.”

Jan shouted from their bedroom.

“HAVE YOU CAUGHT IT YET MIKE?”

"NO, OF COURSE, WE HAVEN’T.”

Mike joined me in the second bedroom where we thought the mouse was hiding. So, forgetting the girls we both turned our full attention to the poor frightened little mouse patiently waiting for us in his new hiding place. As I was the only person in the house who had any knowledge about mice and rats, I again assumed the position of team leader.

I said,

“Mike, are you sure all the doors are shut on the landing?”

He responded,

“Yes, all closed mate”

“OK, good. I suggest you go and open the front door as wide as possible and close all the other doors downstairs."

Mike shot off downstairs carefully following my explicit orders and returned breathlessly.

"All done Geoff."

Now on to plan B in bedroom number two. Having bolted the little blighter once and I must add with no help from Pepper, there shouldn't have been a problem to bolt him out a second time and sure enough, there wasn't.

The tiny brown blur shot through the open bedroom doorway, heading for the stairs.

Instantly, I reacted and dived onto the carpet just as if I was fielding a ball in a game of cricket.

MISSED HIM!

My near miss with the mouse resulted in deafening harmonious screams erupting from the terrified girls who were now clinging to each other on the same chair.

I would have just loved to have frozen that hilarious moment with a photo!

Pepper was sitting on the small landing halfway

down the stairs and was nearly knocked down as Mike and I charged past him in our bid to find out which way 'Speedy' had gone.

I said,

"With a bit of luck, he should have gone outside through the open front door."

But I realised that none of us had seen the highly motivated mouse pass through the open doorway.

Pepper was joined halfway down the stairs by Jan and Kathy. So now we had three spectators.

Mike and I looked around for the little mouse. His only escape route should have been through the open door. There was absolutely no way he could have squeezed under the bottom of any of the other closed doors because they were all flush with the wooden floors. I knew mice could squeeze under very small spaces, but even for our elusive mouse, it looked to be an impossible task.

Pepper seemed to be enjoying the mayhem he had created and sauntered down the stairs to the hallway.

If 'Speedy' hadn't gone through the front door, where the heck was he?

Then I noticed a storage heater up against the hallway wall.

That is when I realised the only hiding place for our little fugitive was the electric storage heater.

'OH, NO! Please not in there! Anywhere but there!'

Mike and I looked at each other and then at the storage heater, both of us hoping that the mouse had not gone inside.

Jan and Kathy braved the scene.

Jan pointed and shouted,

"LOOK! Peppers staring at the heater!"

And yes, that was exactly the direction of Pepper's stare. Well, that appeared to be the only good thing that Pepper had done all night. He had confirmed to us where the mouse was hiding. Mike and I looked down into the back of the heater. And yes, there the poor little chap sat huddled up looking extremely frightened and I am sure more than a little warm.

It was fortunate for our little brown friend that it was not a cold evening and the heater was on very low, in fact, the thermostat had turned it off. We banged and shook the heater.

But 'Speedy' stayed put.

Well, we had no option, but to dismantle the heater, even if it was so late in the evening, we couldn't just leave him in there to maybe fry.

WE HAD TO GET HIM OUT!

I had never taken a storage heater to pieces before and neither had Mike. One o'clock in the morning was not quite the right time to be starting a job like that, especially when you have had a glass of wine or two with a brandy to follow. It's certainly not a job you expect to be doing in the early hours of a Sunday morning in your shirt and tie and in Mike's case.

Now wearing yellow Marigold gloves!

MARIGOLD GLOVES!!!

What the heck!

When did he put those on?

Was he scared of the tiny mouse, or what?

'Are you a man or mouse Mikey?'

Jan and Kathy had been more than brave to creep past the storage heater and the smartly dressed working party. They made their way to the kitchen to make us all a well-deserved drink of hot chocolate. Mike and I were not too impressed that the girls had a shot of brandy in theirs. Especially me because now it looked like I was going to be driving home. With hot mugs cupped in their hands, the girls had finally gotten used to the mad mouse situation and were sitting on the stairs next to Pepper, who couldn't care less what was happening. They were sipping their drinks and chatting happily away whilst keeping a wary eye on the dramatic proceedings. I think they got themselves quite tipsy using the brandy as an excuse to console their shattered nerves.

As the early morning event unfolded, I noticed that Mike and I were very quiet as we worked on the job at hand. I think it was the sheer concentration needed to dismantle that storage heater with all its parts!

Finally, we removed the last panel, yes, at last, that very last panel.

Then we had action...

'Speedy' exploded out at breakneck speed!

Straight at Mike!

Mike's eyes opened wide with shock!

Mike tried to get out of the way!

'Speedy' hit Mike full tilt in the middle of his chest!

'Speedy' bounced off Mike's chest!

Mike went down!

Mike was on his back.

His Marigold gloved hands were flailing the air!

MIKE SCREAMED!

THE GIRLS SCREAMED, IN CRESCENDO!

Mike rolled onto his knees!

The front door was wide open!

'Speedy' ignored it!

BIG MISTAKE!

'Speedy' bolted back towards the hallway!

BIG, BIG MISTAKE!!!

'Speedy' could not get traction on the polished wooden floor!

Mike was back in the game!

Brave Mike scooped 'Speedy' up with his Marigolds!

Mike couldn't hold him!

'Speedy' leapt straight at Mike's forehead!

MIKE SCREAMED!

THE GIRLS SCREAMED, IN CRESCENDO!

'Speedy was tangled in Mike's thick curly hair!

MIKE SCREAMED!

THE GIRLS SCREAMED, IN CRESCENDO!

'Speedy leapt out of Mike's hair!

MIKE SCREAMED!

THE GIRLS SCREAMED, IN CRESCENDO!

'Speedy' headed for the hallway!

BIG MISTAKE!

'Speedy could not get traction!

BIG MISTAKE!

'Speedy' tried to get past me!

BIG, BIG MISTAKE!!!

OH NO!!!

'Speedy' died instantly!

GOT HIM!

I just don't know even to this day why I did it. Perhaps it was pure instinct, or maybe I was just tired, I will never know. The mouse flashed by me and as he did so, I administered a 'Kung Fu' karate chop, that Bruce Lee himself would have been proud of.

Unfortunately, poor old 'Speedy' took the blow amidships.

There was a deathly silence.

You could have heard a pin drop.

I looked around at three accusing faces.

I felt as guilty as a mass murderer!

Jan whispered,

"You've killed him."

"You've killed him."

I tried to defend myself and pleading my innocence I said,

"I thought I was doing the right thing."

Kathy joined in,

"But you didn't have to kill the poor little thing."

"Did you?"

My mate Mike never said a word, he just gave me an accusing look.

With the three of them watching in deathly silence, with guilt and sadness, I picked up the very dead tiny mouse by its tail and carried him outside through the front door that was still wide open and gently laid him in the refuse bin.

I returned back to the three accusing faces, then turned to Mike and said,

“Come on mate. Let’s put this heater back together again.”

In deathly silence, we set about reassembling the heater.

I whispered,

“Women, you can never win with them. Can you?

Mike gave me a wry smile as he handed me a spanner.

It took us three hours to dismantle and put that heater back together again and I won’t tell you what time we went to bed that morning. I will give you a clue, it was daylight.

It was all Peppers's fault he had brought the mouse in.

It was all Peppers's fault that we had chased his not-very-dead mouse all over the house.

It was all Peppers's fault we had to dismantle the heater.

It was all Peppers's fault that Jan was not very happy with me.

It was all Peppers's fault we had lost hours of sleep.

It was all Peppers's fault I got earache from Kathy on the way home for killing the poor little mouse.

As all the excitement was going on, Pepper who couldn't give a 'Monkeys' just sat on the bottom tread of the stairs unconcerned watching the fun. He was not one of my best friends at that time. That's for sure!

Well, of course, I forgave Pepper.

And Jan and Kathy eventually forgave me for taking out the poor unfortunate mouse.

When Mike and Jan took their holidays, a couple next door had a key to their house and were kind enough to feed Pepper and make sure that the cat flap was working. I wonder how many dead or alive trophies of Pepper's they found inside?

As Mike and Jan became more successful in their careers they started to take more holidays. As they were away so often and we owned a cattery, they felt it was unfair to keep relying on their neighbours to look after Pepper.

The good news was that our cattery became Pepper's holiday home.

Jan hated leaving him in a strange environment thinking that he would pine for her. Or more importantly, he was missing his normal freedom of being able to roam wherever he pleased in the beautiful Shropshire countryside outside their house.

Many times, I tried to convince Jan that Pepper enjoyed boarding with us. But, I was sure she didn't believe me. Then I came up with an idea to put her mind at rest and to prove it, I took photos of him in the cattery. I took numerous photos of him lying on his back with all four legs in the air and getting cuddled by the cattery girls.

Jan couldn't believe the photos as he posed there looking so happy. At last, I had convinced her that he never fretted when he stayed with us.

More than often, the cattery girls found body parts of mice which had been unlucky enough to wander into Peppers's run. Bad luck for the mice, but good luck for Pepper. He was far too quick for any of the unfortunate creatures. I am sure none of them ever got away, in the night or even in the day. If mice were brave or stupid enough, they could easily enter the cattery through either of two galvanised steel mesh security doors at each end of the building and freely roam around inside at will. Enticed by the smell of cat food, they were probably trying to rob the cats of any food which they might have left uneaten or any scraps that had fallen on the floor. Unfortunately, for the mice, it was not quite like the Tom and Jerry cartoons, where Jerry always survived. I am afraid that the little mice could never win in our feline paradise, they didn't stand a chance, especially if most of the cats were as quick as Pepper. The cats didn't even have to use any of their precious energy hunting, because the live food was delivered to them free of charge and as fresh as it possibly could get. You could say, 'It was meals on legs'. I even took my camera into Peppers run first thing one morning, to take a photograph to show Jan the remains of one of his night-time feasts.

With Pepper boarding with us on a regular basis, he soon became one of the favourites of all the cattery staff. He loved lying on his back and having his tummy tickled and that big booming purr of his was released enthusiastically from within his heaving rib cage.

Due to our relationship with Mike and Jan, we were invited to many Law Society dinners, which was a rare chance for me to dress up and wear a dinner jacket and bow tie, very unlike my daily dress, a Barbour jacket, blue faded jeans and green wellies.

Over the years, we met a lot of partners and staff from Mike's firm and also from Jan's work with the County Council. Most of them had pets and used our cattery and kennels on a regular basis. All this trade stemmed from our good friends Mike and Jan. And of course, not forgetting the legendary Pepper, especially after his cattery portfolio was revealed to Mike and Jan’s friends and work associates. Also, we pinned photos of Pepper on our large notice board in our reception/office for all to see. For sure, you can’t beat a bit of good old advertising!

So, thank you, my ginger mate, Pepper the trophy hunter.

More of Geoff's alarming but interesting facts about wild rabbits

With me being a nature lover, I thought after that amusing story about Pepper and his rabbit trophy, this would be a perfect opportunity to reveal the alarming facts about the plight of the poor rabbit in the 1950s. If you are squeamish, maybe you should bypass the next two paragraphs and move on to some laughter.

The disgusting virus myxomatosis was created by man and transmitted primarily by insects. Disease transmission commonly occurs via mosquito or flea bites, but can also occur via the bites of mites, flies, and lice. The myxoma virus does not replicate in these insect hosts but is physically carried by biting insects from one rabbit to another. Seasonally it is driven by the availability of insect vectors (an organism, typically a biting insect or tick, which transmits a disease or parasite from one animal or plant to another) and the proximity of infected wild rabbits. The myxoma virus can also be transmitted by direct contact. Infected rabbits shed the virus in ocular and nasal secretions and from eroded skin lesions. The virus may also be present in semen and genital secretions. Poxviruses are fairly stable in the environment and can be spread by contaminated objects such as water bottles, feeders, cages, or people's hands. They are resistant to drying but are sensitive to some disinfectants.

In Australia, in 1950 the disease was deliberately released at full scale. Nobody would believe what happened next. The myxomatosis turned out to be devastatingly effective, reducing the rabbits from 600 million at that point to 100 million in the course of a two-year period. It was also introduced in France in the 1950s to control the wild European rabbit population. It became the cause of death for ninety per cent of the wild rabbits in the country. From there, myxomatosis further spread throughout Europe too. In the UK, the disease was encouraged in 1953 as a means of effective biological control measures. The outbreak was so severe that it is deemed to have been the cause of death to almost ninety-nine per cent of the rabbits on the island!

Well, that's enough of the serious stuff.

Here comes the laughter...

CHAPTER 2

An Indian Take-Away

Here we have a bit of a drama featuring two cats, ending with a scorching (scorching is the operative word) hilarious climax.

This is a tale about two cats from the large West Midlands town of Wolverhampton. The cats are named, Fluffy and Teddy.

For sure, their names certainly described their appearances and characters.

Fluffy was a small female cat with long black fluffy fur. Peeping out of her fluffy face were two gorgeous yellow eyes, and she was a non-stop purrer.

Teddy was a male cat with short light brown fur, and two white front feet, which gave you the impression he had a pair of white gloves on. He most certainly resembled a Teddy bear, hence his name. In my opinion, he had some Burmese in him. I have always found these breeds quite friendly, and Teddy was certainly no exception.

When Fluffy and Teddy came to stay with us,

our business was two years down the road and well-established. I was employing quite a few staff and also a manager named Pat. We found Fridays, Saturdays, Sundays, and Mondays to be our busiest days with customers delivering and collecting.

Fortunately for us, there were numerous school children (mostly girls) available who wanted to work with animals and we were inundated with phone calls asking for jobs, or in some cases, even volunteering to work for free! The girls absolutely loved their work, and as a bonus for us, they were available throughout their school holidays.

They even volunteered to work on Christmas Day and Boxing Day!

This was a wonderful arrangement for both parties because our busiest times always revolved around school holidays. Most of the girls and the occasional boy were very good at working with the cats and dogs and needed very little supervision. Their ages ranged from twelve to sixteen and worked conscientiously like responsible adults rather than children.

Now back to Fluffy and Teddy.

Fluffy and Teddy were delivered on a Saturday morning. As usual, we went through our routine of checking vaccination certificates and any special requirements before the cats were taken from their owner's car. The two cats were handed to us in their separate carriers, which we put on the office floor.

I raised my eyebrows when I saw the type of containers the two cats were in!

Fluffy and Teddy were booked in for exactly two weeks. Their owners asked me if it would be okay for a neighbour to collect them because they would not be arriving home until late in the evening. I confirmed that it would be in order as long as their friend proved who he was and paid when he collected. The owners felt it would be far simpler if they paid in advance that day, rather than complicating things later. So they did and gave me their friend's name and telephone number.

Having sorted everything out, the owners left us to take Fluffy and Teddy down to the cattery.

Cat containers came in all shapes and sizes. They could be plastic boxes, cane baskets, plastic-coated wire, wood, cardboard and even some strange homemade ones.

Take note, Fluffy and Teddy had arrived in cardboard carriers.

Besides cardboard carriers being insecure, the cats within cannot see out, therefore they would be travelling in the dark, which is far from ideal. Surely cats would like to see where they are going.

So, now you have probably got the gist that I definitely do not like cardboard carriers one little bit!

And that is the essence of this story!

The cardboard carriers that Fluffy and Teddy arrived in had most certainly seen a few years of use that resulted in the cardboard being extremely pliable. This meant that if the two cats were left unattended, there was a possibility that they could push themselves out. Also, if either of the cardboard containers were picked up by the handle, the fragile bottom could be weak and Teddy or Fluffy could drop out. Not only might one of them injure itself, but there was a strong possibility that one or both might be frightened by the experience and bolt into the one hundred acres of woodland that surrounded our property.

So, now you know why I raised my eyebrows.

Having examined the awful state of the two containers holding Fluffy and Teddy, I instructed two of my most experienced girls on how I wanted them to hold and carry the containers down to the cattery. I asked them to be very careful by holding the handle on the top with one hand and the other hand underneath securing the bottom. Trusting the two girls to do what they had done dozens of times before. I left them to it and returned to the office to pick up the ringing telephone. I hadn't been on the phone for many seconds when I heard a loud scream…

It had come from one of the girls on the way to the cattery.

Then one of them shouted,

"GEOFF, GEOFF, COME QUICK!!!"

I reacted instantly and dropped the phone like a lump of red hot coal into the hands of Pat my manager who had just entered the office. I left her to continue my conversation with a customer on the other end who must have been wondering what was going on.

I shot outside and was mortified to see the two girls rooted to the spot.

They were standing in the middle of the lawn halfway between the office and the cattery.

To my horror, one of the cats was walking toward me, leaving one of the girls holding the cardboard container by the handle, with the useless bottom hanging down.

My main concern was not to alarm the cat. The cat didn't know me and it could easily panic and shoot off into the surrounding woodland, never to be seen again.

My thoughts were,

'This is the first time this cat has visited us and I hope it isn't going to be the last!'

I called softly to the two girls to stay still, not to panic and just leave it to me.

I slowly walked up to the cat, which turned out to be Teddy and with no trouble at all I stroked him and picked him up. Teddy was so lovable, just purring away, appearing not to be the slightest bit bothered that he was in a stranger's arms. I think he was probably just glad to be out of the dark old dilapidated cardboard container.

Cradling Teddy in my arms, I walked slowly down to the cattery and the two girls safely installed him with Fluffy in one of the spacious runs.

No harm done!

PHEW…

WERE WE LUCKY, OR WHAT?

During Teddy's unpredicted rescue, I had the horrible thought of explaining to his owners just why Teddy preferred to live in the woodland rather than our luxurious cattery. And would they mind going into the woods to search for him?

Thank goodness, that was not the case!

The member of staff whose name I will never reveal learned from her mistake. After her frightening experience, she turned out to be one of our very best girls and lucky for us, stayed with us for many years afterwards.

What the heck has all this got to do with an

Indian take-away, you might well ask?

Well, here it comes...

Fluffy and Teddy spent an enjoyable time with us and all the staff loved them as they were both so incredibly cuddly and friendly. It was a Saturday when their owner's friend turned up to collect them. And he just happened to be an Indian gentleman who introduced himself as Rahji.

Now, we are getting to the title of this chapter.

Rahji arrived in a gleaming dark blue Jaguar saloon. He looked very distinguished in his made-to-measure grey pin-striped suit, a crisp white shirt and blue tie. I thought he looked impeccable. He had the look of a doctor, lawyer, or most probably he owned a string of Indian restaurants.

He certainly didn't look suitably dressed for collecting and cuddling two cats!

I instructed the same pair of girls from Teddy's earlier drama to bring the two cats up from the cattery because I knew that they would do anything to avoid a repeat performance. When the gang of four eventually arrived outside the office, I asked them to put the cardboard carriers directly into Rahji's car, rather than bring them into the office which was our normal procedure.

I wanted the two cats in Rahji's car, ASAP.

We certainly didn't want the same scenario happening again.

I feared the next time, we might not be so lucky!

In the meantime, Rahji was sitting in my office explaining to me how terrified he was of cats and looking at his face I could see he had a genuine fear of them.

He said,

"If a cat just looks at me I go into a hot sweat."

'Why have the owners asked this guy to collect their cats?'

I explained to him that he didn't have anything to worry about because Fluffy and Teddy were enclosed in cat containers and he wouldn't even be able to see them. And even better, they wouldn't be able to see him. I could see he was a bit more settled with my comforting words.

Suddenly, his face turned a whiter shade of pale

and beads of sweat appeared on his forehead. I looked past him to find out what was troubling him. Lo and behold, he was looking in horror at the flimsy cardboard containers which were being carried to his car by my two girls.

To make the cardboard containers more secure, we bound them with copious amounts of blue bailing twine.

Rahji was looking at the two flimsy cardboard box-like containers wrapped in blue bailing twine.

They were carrying horrible cats!

What?

Blue bailing twine?

Not very professional!

Not professional at all!

RAHJI, WAS NOT HAPPY!

NOT HAPPY AT ALL!

With widened eyes, he ran over to his car. He looked down at the two old containers with both of the weakened cardboard tops moving up and down from the pressure inflicted by the cats inside.

He pleaded,

“I am not having them in my car. Please, please put them in the boot?”

Unfortunately for him, or should I say his peace of mind, we had to insist each cardboard container went behind the front seats in the rear foot-wells. I explained that the containers would be more stable there and wouldn’t be thrown about, as they would have been in the car boot.

With great hesitation, he accepted my explanation and let us load them in the rear footwells of his luxurious Jaguar.

Before Rahji got into the Jaguar, tentatively he peered through the side window and he could see the top of one of the containers moving up and down. The girls and I knew that it was Teddy pushing and rubbing his head under the flimsy cardboard top almost as if he was being stroked.

I looked into the poor guy’s face, the whites of his eyes appeared to be rolling and his face was ashen.

I tried to explain that they were very, very friendly cats and they wouldn't harm him in any way at all. But I could see I was fighting a losing battle.

And more alarmingly, so was the cardboard container holding Teddy!

I said,

"Don't worry, it won't take long for you to get back to Wolverhampton."

With eyes wide open he replied.

"You bet it won't!"

With that, he leapt into his car.

He fired up the powerful engine of the Jaguar and with screeching tyres, he was gone in a flash, leaving us to cope with the smell of burning rubber and exhaust fumes.

I said to the two girls standing by me,

"He's just made a Formula One driver look like a tortoise on the starting grid."

I joked,

“If I drive fast to Wolverhampton, I can get there in twenty minutes.”

“This guy is going to do it in ten!”

The girls burst into laughter.

I joked again,

“If those cats break out of their containers, I wouldn’t like to be in his wife’s shoes washing his underwear!”

We certainly had a good laugh about it and knew it would have been a miracle if the two cardboard containers had held together all the way to Wolverhampton.

I must say, we did feel a little guilty toward him, but we were only doing what was best for our friends, Fluffy and Teddy. We sincerely hoped that they wouldn't manage to break out because they could have caused a bad accident. I had asked him to phone me at his journey's end because of my concern for him and his two furry passengers.

Fortunately, he rang me twenty minutes later with the welcoming news that the three of them had arrived safely.

Fluffy and Teddy became regular guests of ours, and that is how we picked up from their owners the ending of this story.

When Rahji got back, he vacated his smart Jaguar at speed, and left Fluffy and Teddy to it. He was frightened to go anywhere near them, let alone touch them. Unfortunately, Fluffy and Teddy's owners were delayed and within that time Fluffy and Teddy managed to break out of their boxes. Waiting for their owners they made themselves well and truly at home, unfortunately, leaving cat hairs everywhere.

When Fluffy and Teddy's owners went to Rahji's home they found the Jaguar unlocked in the driveway, with no sign of the driver. They looked inside and could see the two cats fast asleep cuddled blissfully together on the cream leather driving seat.

The two harmless cats hadn't experienced any trauma at all, unlike their Indian friend who very nearly had a nervous breakdown.

The sleek Jaguar was sold within weeks of Fluffy and Teddy's luxurious sleep. I am sure someone must have had a bargain!

And surprise, surprise, Rahji did own an Indian restaurant.

And he never collected Fluffy and Teddy again.

In conclusion, I can't understand why someone should ask a friend to collect cats when he is obviously terrified of them. He must have been an extremely good friend or possibly he hadn't informed them of his tremendous fear of cats. Or maybe he owed them a favour.

If that was the case, it must have been a very big favour.

Anyway, we knew that there was one cat that Rahji did like.

The Jaguar!

Not surprisingly, the Jags scorched tyre marks remained on the tarmac surface of our car park for a considerable time.

Reminding us of...

A rubber-burning, Indian Take-Away!!!

CHAPTER 3

The Yellow Monster

This is a humorous white-knuckle story giving you an idea of how traumatic running our business could be.

Loss of life comes to mind!

Our pet boarding business had been operating successfully for three years. This story took place in the fourth year when we had the wettest June and July ever recorded. The heavens opened up making it quite miserable and difficult to work with our furry canine guests. The cats were okay because they were well protected inside the cattery building from any type of inclement weather.

During our twice-daily dog walking sessions, it certainly was not fun tramping around a sodden, muddy woodland circuit. The poor dogs never seemed to dry out, although they never seemed to mind, and trying to keep their bedding dry was an absolute nightmare.

And things got worse.

Much, much worse!

It was 7.30 am on a cold wet July Sunday morning when I got the shock of my life.

As I entered the original showpiece kennel block, (two more buildings were added later). I was gobsmacked when I found every single run flooded with rainwater.

I couldn't believe what I was looking at.

'Arghhh!'

All the dogs were standing in six inches of water.

It was heartbreaking to see the dogs looking so terribly forlorn.

There were twenty-two kennels in the block, with large runs measuring 10 x 6 feet, separated by four-foot walls painted light green and topped with silver galvanised steel mesh. The cosy sleeping quarters measuring 6 x 6 feet situated at the far end of each run were heated by infrared lamps. The lamps were suspended on stainless steel chains hanging from six-foot-high ceilings.

Did we spoil our furry guests, or what?

The entrance to each concrete run had a

galvanised steel mesh gate with a four-inch ground clearance. Luckily, none of the sleeping quarters had flooded because I had designed a slight fall. The fall was ideal for daily hosing with our pressure washer. The smart sleeping quarters had red terracotta tiled floors laid by me. The tiles created a lip that stopped water from backwashing inside. The clearance under the mesh gate allowed water from the power washer to flow underneath into a long gully. The gully stretched along the front of the runs and emptied into a drain on the outside of the kennel building by the office and car park. Therefore, the flood water in the runs was at its deepest by the mesh gates and never reached the sleeping quarters.

At least that was one blessing on that memorable miserable day.

I found the situation unbelievable because all of our buildings were situated on top of a small hill.

So how had it flooded?

When I first inspected the submerged grid at the end of the gully, I thought it was blocked by dog hairs or leaves that could have blown from the silver birch spinney bordering our car park. So, all I had to do was remove the offending debris allowing the flood water to rapidly drain away.

WRONG!

The bad news was that it was not the grid that was blocked, it turned out to be the underground soak-away.

I could not believe it!

The soak-away was designed to take away the rainwater running from the roof of the large kennel block. I must admit, it was a tremendous amount of water. I had installed the soak-away myself, and when I do a job, I do a good job and I had made doubly sure that I had taken excessive rainfall into consideration.

The subterranean soak-away was a trench twenty-five yards long by six feet wide, it had a depth of six feet and was filled with clean used building bricks. And that is standard procedure for making a soak-away. The soak-away ran away from the original kennel block, alongside the car park and was lurking under my beautiful large lush lawn.

The last thing I wanted was to dig that up!

But how was I going to release the floodwater

that the wretched dogs were standing in?

I had no choice.

A hole had to be dug.

A big one!

And not by hand either.

I needed a JCB excavator.

I needed one quick!

And the unrelenting rain continued to come down in buckets and buckets.

Have you ever noticed that it's always on a Sunday when you need something urgently?

So, where on earth was I going to get a JCB with a driver on a Sunday?

Well, I racked my brains like never before. I thumbed through the good old Yellow Pages like a blur, and the irritatingly persistent rain was still streaming down in torrents. All the contractors I phoned were very sympathetic, but with it being Sunday they couldn't help me because all the lucky chaps had the day off. And I bet my bottom dollar they were not going to church either.

More than likely the pub!

So what the heck was I going to do?

Then it came to me. The previous year, I had noticed that one of the local farmers, John Whitfield had an old JCB parked in an open barn. I was at John's farm because he had phoned me regarding a big problem. There was a fox raiding his hen house killing some of the chickens within.

He was very lucky it was not all of them!

With me being an ex-gamekeeper, 'Mr Charlie Fox' (a country nickname) was an old adversary of mine. Take note, foxes kill pheasants in vast numbers when they manage to infiltrate a breeding pen.

I had gone over to John's farm to look at the problem and give him some advice on how to avoid future raids by cunning Charlie.

The dilapidated old henhouse was built with wooden boards and was in dire need of repair. Watched by John, it was not long before I found the gap between the boards where Charlie had squeezed through to commit his multiple murders. Unbelievingly, it was four feet off the ground and so small that you wouldn't think a squirrel could squeeze through, let alone a cunning fox.

But it had!

To prove it, I grabbed a small tuft of fox fur that was attached to the rough wood on the edge of the gap. I held the fur up between my thumb and index finger for John to see.

He was amazed.

I advised John to strengthen the henhouse by banging in numerous small panels and plenty of nails to patch up any gaps. Also, to rig an electric cattle fence nine inches above the ground surface surrounding the henhouse, which he did. (This electric fence method is standard procedure in gamekeeping.) Hence, saving the remaining chickens from a frightening violent death!

Mr Charlie fox

A fox fact

After a fox raid, many of the dead chickens are totally unmarked. The reason is that the terrified panic-stricken chickens just drop dead with fright!

John was overjoyed with my detective work and knowledgeable advice.

He said,

"Geoff, if ever I can do you a favour, please don't hesitate to ask."

AND THEY DON'T COME MUCH BIGGER THAN A JCB!

On that dreadful wet day, I phoned John and it rang for quite a long time. As I clung to the phone, I hoped and prayed that he was at the farmhouse. Eventually, he picked up, and to cut a long story short, within the hour, I heard the powerful machine coming up our quarter-mile drive that threaded through the Scots pine woodland.

To my relief, with John at the helm, the big yellow JCB roared onto the car park.

To fix the floodwater problem we needed to dig a large hole. Unfortunately, and that word is a massive understatement, the hole needed to be dug in our beautiful landscaped lawn that expanded from the car park down to the cattery and our cottage a hundred and thirty yards away.

The sad news was, the unsightly gaping hole would only be a few feet from our office come reception room for all the customers to see as they entered.

'ARGHHH!'

After a brief discussion, we decided how big the hole needed to be.

With that, John climbed into the cab of the JCB and the Yellow Monster roared.

I watched in dismay, as the powerful machine ripped into my beautiful green turf, just as if it was a sponge cake coated with green icing.

In a later very amusing chapter about a Chinese lady, you will see just how hard we worked to achieve such a beautiful lawn.

I could have cried!

But, the machine had to do, what a machine had to do.

After two hours of ripping, tearing and digging, there was an ugly gaping hole twenty feet square with a depth of ten feet. This resulted in a horrible unsightly mountain of muddy soil that all our customers were going to see, piled high, smothering what was once part of my beautiful hand-sewn lawn.

As much as I wanted to, I never shed a tear.

With my trusty spade, Geoff the human JCB quickly dug a shallow trench from the grid of the flooded gully to the gaping hole. To my relief, and I am sure all the dogs as well, my digging rapidly released the floodwater from the kennel building.

The horrible gaping hole had taken longer to dig than John had envisaged and with his farm being two miles away, chugging back in the old JCB was going to take him quite some time. He was in a big hurry to get back for milking, so he asked me if he could leave the JCB on our car park and he would come and pick it up another day. I agreed, so John parked the JCB about twenty yards away from the office and gave me the keys just in case I needed to move it. So, with that in mind, I ran him back to his farm in my light green Daihatsu Jeep 4x4. Unfortunately, the JCB stood on our small car park for almost two weeks. It was taking up two precious parking spaces and I thought it was going to take root.

After numerous phone calls to John, he could not find the time to come and pick it up.

Sunday, two weeks later, Kathy's parents came

over for the day. Kathy's dad Ronnie was a thick-set, ruddy-faced farmer and her mum Isabelle pale and frail in comparison. They lived in the neighbouring county of Cheshire. They loved to drive to Shropshire and see what we were up to. And we enjoyed having them.

So I had an idea…

With Ronnie being here, why not make use of him?

Here comes the idea…

Maybe we could take the old machine back ourselves?

OLD, being the operative word!

I phoned John yet again to see if he could drive away the JCB, which by now was seriously getting on my nerves cluttering up the car park. Again, he didn't have time, so I suggested perhaps I could drive it back myself, which he immediately agreed to.

Well, I must admit, I did fancy the idea of driving the big machine and with Ronnie the farmer being here, it made good sense.

I took note of John's words,

"She can be a stubborn old sod at times. But, you should have no problem managing her. Just be careful if you put her in third gear because sometimes it jams and you can't get it out."

This sounded a bit like a recipe for disaster, so I assured John that I was DEFINITELY going to keep well away from third gear.

Five minutes before my exciting trip, Ronnie and I stood by our back garden fence and I pointed to John's farm, a dot in the distance. The plan was for Ronnie to lead the way driving my Daihatsu Jeep and I would follow in the big Yellow Monster.

Jesus, did I say exciting?

So, off Ronnie and I strolled from our cottage across the long soggy lawn up to the car park where the imposing old machine was waiting for me. I climbed up the steps to the high cab, climbed inside and sat in the driving seat. Ronnie climbed up, stood on the top steel step then peered inside.

We carefully studied the controls.

With Ronnie being used to farm machinery, the controls of the old JCB were quite familiar. They were not that much different from his tractors. Also, I had driven quite a few tractors in my time. So between us, we had no trouble understanding the big machine's setup.

Inserting the ignition key, I turned it and the old faithful beast fired into life. The big, powerful diesel engine roared as Ronnie jumped down from the cab.

After digesting Ronnie's previous instructions, tentatively I moved one of the control levers and the massive front bucket started to rise high in the air where I left it raised. This action enabled me to see underneath so I could see where I was going.

Thankfully, most of the way to the farm was across fields, only about a quarter of the ensuing journey was on a narrow country tarmac lane. I thought it would be safer for any on-coming vehicles if Ronnie with the Jeep's headlights shining brightly went first, warning unwary drivers that a big wide Yellow Monster was...

APPROACHING...

WITH A NOVICE DRIVER!

So, off we set on our exciting adventure.

And this is where the real fun starts!

I put the old machine into first gear, me and my new yellow mate chugged off.

Exiting the car park, we made a left onto our tarmac drive. Following the drive for seventy yards or so it curled left. To our right, we passed the front of our picturesque mauve sandstone cottage with its wooden garden gate enclosed by a dense green lovely beech hedge. Ten yards on, situated on our left we passed the long, stone-coloured, single-storey cattery building with its corrugated green fibreglass roof.

Leaving our drive we entered the bordering oak woodland onto a short stoney track. Still, in first gear, we chugged along the track that turned out to be a little bumpy exaggerated by the machine's hard suspension. After five long minutes, we emerged onto a large barley stubble field that belonged to David Craddock a neighbouring farmer. Ronnie in the Jeep was waiting on the stubble field forty yards or so away. He gave me the thumbs up, so I returned the gesture and we started across the field.

But, the JCB was moving too slowly.

And I mean far too slowly!

'We need to speed up.'

Engaging second gear became a better option.

So, I did and we did a little lurch forward.

I slowly chugged after Ronnie down the side of the stubble field, at a speed that I can only describe as...

VERY, VERY SLOW!

A snail could have sped past me.

I thought,

'It's going to take us forever to get to John's farm at this pace.'

'Stuff it, 'No guts, no glory'.'

'I'll risk third gear!'

BIG, BIG, MISTAKE!

In the past, I had driven many powerful sports cars. So, how on earth could a big lumbering beast such as a JCB frighten me?

Would these be my famous last words?

I engaged third gear...

'HELP ME!'

The old Yellow Monster shot forward with a frightening, accelerating lurch.

To my horror...

I was gaining rapidly on Ronnie!

AND, I MEAN RAPIDLY!

Ronnie, with not a care in the world, was happily tootling along...

He had no idea what was happening behind him.

THE YELLOW MONSTER WAS REELING HIM IN!

IT WANTS TO KILL HIM!!!

The awesome machine, threatening Ronnie was

lurching and wallowing dangerously on the uneven ground of the stubble field. To say it was unstable was no exaggeration.

I, who generally feared nothing behind a steering wheel, was frightened out of my wits.

Immediately, I decided that third gear was not such a good idea after all. So I attempted to knock it out and put it back into second.

'OH NO!'

It won't budge!

And the revs mysteriously increased.

IT WAS JAMMED!!!

ARGHHH!!!

The stubborn brute, with a mind of its own, decided it preferred third gear and keep up the revs.

I braked hard.

Nothing happened.

Nothing at all.

No brakes?

'Oh no!'

The brakes aren't working.

ARGHHH!!!

And the clutch must have gone on holiday too!

As strong as I was, even with both hands, I couldn't budge the jammed old gear stick.

I looked out the side of the cab.

I could see I had two choices.

Flattening Ronnie!!!

OR...

TAKE EVASIVE ACTION!

I TOOK EVASIVE ACTION!

I wrenched the big steering wheel to the left.

The powerful machine bounced and lurched.

It was out of control!

I WAS OUT OF CONTROL!

'I'm going to die.'

ARGHHH!!!

'OH, NO! This thing is going to turn over!'

Luckily it was my stomach that turned over not the machine!

I tried to fight the steering wheel.

I WAS LOSING!

MY KNUCKLES WERE WHITE!

The Yellow Monster containing its terrified passenger, went roaring past Ronnie.

I MISSED HIM BY A HAIR'S BREADTH!

I glanced at him as I…

ROARED BY!

As I shot past Ronnie he looked up at me, and

to say he had a surprised look on his face would have been a gross understatement. His normally healthy ruddy red face had turned ghostly white and his eyes stood out like organ stops.

His jaw dropped wide open as if to say,

'What is that madman trying to do?'

The Yellow Monster lurched, wallowed and bucked onward with its terrified passenger desperately clinging onto the steering wheel.

Ronnie decided to give chase and find out why on earth his son-in-law had decided to take up rallying in a JCB.

The least of my problems was Ronnie!

My thoughts had definitely turned to the self-preservation variety.

The initial journey across the stubble field was on a slight incline, but I knew at the top of the rise, there lurked a long steep decline.

My fears were rising even more as the awesome yellow beast still chose to keep the revs up and stay stubbornly...

JAMMED IN THIRD GEAR!

AND THE BRAKES WERE INEFFECTIVE!

Over the rise the Yellow Monster exploded, spraying mud on the little green Jeep following close behind.

Unsurprisingly, Ronnie decided no way was he going to pull level with the violently swerving madman in case he flattened him to a pulp.

I thought the monstrous machine was bad enough to handle when it was going up the slight incline, but trying to control it downhill was an entirely different education.

On my more than exciting journey across the stubble field, I haven't mentioned what effect the front bucket was having.

Well, I am sure most people know a JCB has a massive bucket on the front and a smaller bucket on an extending arm at the back.

The smaller one on the back, which was swinging to and fro created the machine to violently sway.

The eight feet wide lump of steel on the front of the monstrous yellow beast was raised high in the sky fighting against gravity.

And losing!

The massive bucket was bouncing up and down making the machine totally unstable.

'OH NO! I'm going to die!'

It occurred to me that the Yellow Monster had ambitions of its own.

Somersaulting all the way down the hill came to mind!

I wrestled with the big steering wheel.

I tried to knock the machine out of gear.

It suddenly dawned on me…

When me and my yellow mate run out of stubble field...

Waiting for us at the bottom...

Was...

A NARROW TRACK!

ARGHHH!!!

This was not good news!

Because…

The track had a sharp right-hand bend.

And a left-hand bend.

Followed by a narrow steel bridge with handrails spanning a small river.

The river Meese.

I was in a cold sweat.

'OH NO!'

'I'm going for a Sunday afternoon swim!'

'Shall I bail out?'

'NO!'

I clung on in terror.

I took the right-hand bend.

I took the left-hand bend.

And made it.

'PHEW!'

'A MIRACLE!'

How I survived those bends I will never know.

But…

'OH NO!'

The bridge and river are looming up fast.

'TOO FAST!'

We thundered on.

The narrow bridge was close.

Too close!

THE MONSTER ROARED!!!

We thundered on.

THE MONSTER ROARED!!!

We hit the steel floor of the bridge.

CLATTER, CLATTER!

THE MONSTER ROARED!!!

CLATTER, CLATTER!

We almost took out the flimsy steel handrails.

CLATTER, CLATTER!

THE MONSTER ROARED!!!

CLATTER, CLATTER!

We were over.

I was still alive.

'PHEWWW!'

Having clattered over the bridge at a speed that I would have never contemplated in a Ferrari, my troubles were not over.

Not by a long shot!

A bumpy, steep hill was approaching.

APPROACHING FAST!

WAY, WAY TOO FAST!

THE MONSTER ROARED!!!

We lurched, we rolled.

THE MONSTER ROARED!!!

We thundered on.

A very narrow, busy country lane at the top of the hill was approaching fast.

Way, way too fast.

COLD SWEAT!

I was at the end of my tether.

COLD SWEAT!

'We're eating up the ground!'

COLD SWEAT!

'We're going way too fast!'

COLD SWEAT!

'We're getting closer to the busy lane!'

COLD, COLD SWEAT!

Everyone knows that narrow country lanes have cars.

Tiny cars that contain vulnerable soft-skinned humans.

The Yellow Monster was not going to take any prisoners.

KILL THEM ALL!!!

COLD SWEAT!

KILL THEM ALL!!!

COLD, COLD SWEAT!

The Yellow Monster lumbered and lurched as we thundered up the hill, I had thoughts on my mind of me becoming famous for…

CAUSING…

A SHROPSHIRE MASSACRE!

NEWS HEADLINES
PET HOTEL PROPRIETOR GOES BERSERK
DRIVING A MONSTER JCB
FLATTENING FIFTEEN CARS CONTAINING NUMEROUS OCCUPANTS!

In sheer desperation, I let go of the steering wheel, stood up and with all my strength using two hands I attempted to shift the Yellow Monster's gear stick.

IT POPPED OUT!

I grabbed the steering wheel.

I hit the brakes.

Thank goodness they worked.

The roaring Monster ground to a halt.

The little Jeep ground to a halt.

My heart virtually ground to a halt.

I wiped the cold beads of sweat off my brow.

Ronnie climbed up to the Yellow Monster's cab.

In fits of laughter.

He said,

"What have you been playing at?"

"Are you crazy?"

"Or what?"

I was absolutely speechless. I tried to regain my senses and gradually my heart thankfully slowed down from its frightening frantic pace to a steady beat.

Having miraculously survived the ordeal, (with unsoiled underpants) there was absolutely no way I was going to risk engaging third gear for the final leg of that frightening journey.

No way!

No way at all!

It must have aged me by ten years.

I didn't care how long it was going to take. Two days came to mind!

I WAS STILL ALIVE!

I decided to complete the rest of the journey in second gear. The amazing thing was, as we chugged through those country lanes, we never met a single car.

I bet you, if I had still been stuck in third gear, the lane would have been teeming.

At long last we arrived at the farm and were greeted by a smiling John.

He said,

"Well, how did you get on driving the old girl?"

As I replied, I looked at Ronnie and winked.

"A piece of cake mate."

Later that day Ronnie through more fits of laughter said,

"When I saw you trying to take those bends and the bridge at suicidal speed, I really thought you were going into the river. I could hardly drive the jeep I was roaring with laughter so much."

I responded,

"I don't know, the things I do to keep our furry guests happy."

I bet you are wondering what happened to the ugly hole in my lovely lawn. Well, I decided to leave it there for a while, just in case any more delightful deluges of rainfall decided to attack our canine guests again.

After a few weeks, the UGLY hole was filled in by John and the behaving Yellow Monster. I am sure the spotlight perched on the top of the yellow cab winked at me! I can assure you, after experiencing that imaginary wink by the spotlight, I stayed well clear while John was doing the work.

My lovely lawn was eventually restored to its former glory with a few handfuls of grass seed and a little help from Mother Nature. I solved the problem of future flooding by running the surface gulley in the opposite direction from the kennel building, channelling the rainwater to soak away naturally in a quiet part of the woodland.

I was ecstatic John had the time to take the old Yellow Monster home because I wouldn't have cared if it was sitting on the car park for months and taken root. There was no way I was climbing into that Yellow Monsters cab again!

I decided that my little red Wheelhorse ride-on-mower was just a little bit more tranquil to ride on!

CHAPTER 4

Fun in the Woods

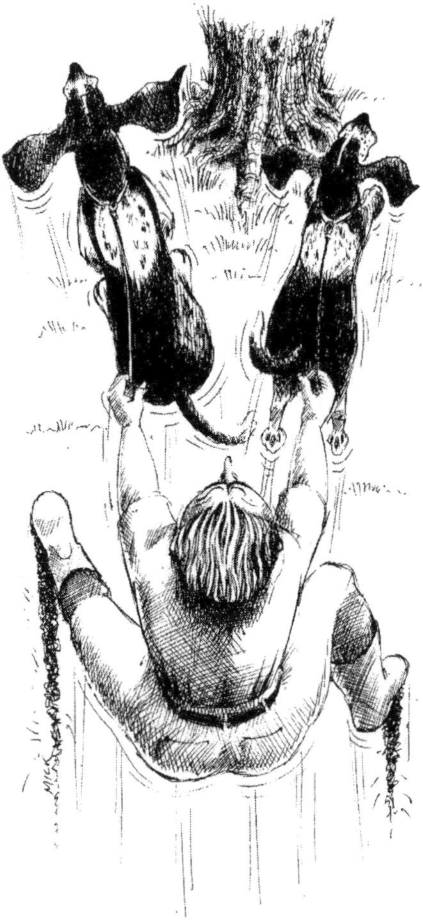

Harry and Henry

Fun in the woods! Now that is questionable.

Dog walking could be great fun and we certainly had lots of laughs over the years, as you will see in these next stories.

Harriett and Henrietta were two Basset Hounds, both were bitches as their names suggest, but were called Harry and Henry for short. Both of them were definitely from the same mould and had incredible characters, well they were sisters after all.

In my experience, Basset Hounds have similar characters that can only be described as...

SERIOUSLY, SERIOUSLY STUBBORN!!!

Here are some facts relating to this story.

Fact

The Basset Hound is a short-legged breed of

dog from the Hound family. The Basset is a scent Hound that was originally bred for the purpose of hunting hares. Their sense of smell and their ability to ground scent is second only to the Bloodhound. Basset Hounds are one of six recognised 'Basset' - type breeds in France. The name Basset is derived from the French word 'bas', meaning low, with the attenuating suffix 'et' together meaning 'rather low'. Basset Hounds are usually bi-colours or tri-colours of standard hound colouration. Generally black, white and tan (tri-colour) or tan/lemon and white (bi-colour), but any recognised hound colour is acceptable.

Bassets are large, short, solid and long, with curved sabre tails held high over their long backs. An adult male dog weighs: 25–34 kg (55–75 pounds) female: 20–29 kg (45–65 pounds).

Male's height: 30–38 cm (12–15 inches) female: 28–36 cm (11–14 inches) This breed, relative to its size, is heavier-boned than any other dog and very, very strong, **as you will soon realise in this story.**

The Basset, like its ancestor the Bloodhound, has a hanging skin structure, which causes the face to occasionally look sad. This, for many people, adds to the breed's charm. The dewlap, (a fold of loose skin hanging from the neck or throat of an animal) is seen as the loose, elastic skin around the neck, and the trailing ears, which, along with the Bloodhound are the longest of any breed, help trap the scent of what they are tracking. Its neck is wider than its head. This combined with the loose skin around its face and neck means that flat collars can easily be pulled off. The looseness of the skin results in Basset's characteristic facial wrinkles. They drool a lot due to the loose skin around their mouths.

The Basset Hound is a friendly, outgoing, and playful dog, tolerant of children and other pets. They are extremely vocal and famously devoted to tracking. They are also widely known for being stubborn. **Prospective owners must be prepared to handle Bassets firmly and patiently.**

That last sentence will certainly help you to

appreciate the following events.

Have you ever tried to walk a Basset Hound on a lead?

Absolutely impossible, I can assure you of that.

And I tried to walk two!

I had never met a Basset Hound before Harry and Henry boarded with us, and boy, I never realised I was in for a big, big education.

Basset Hounds are a breed that I will never forget for many reasons.

I can only describe their voice as a mournful baying sound, which is emitted from deep inside their broad barrel-shaped ribcage. This baying sound usually happened when they picked up the scent of a hare, rabbit or food. I suppose hares, rabbits and food are one and the same to a Basset. I can tell you they got seriously excited about all of them!

And those last words certainly relate to this story!

Not only do Bassets have immense power and strength, but they also have massive paws at the end of their short stumpy legs. I was the first person on our premises that attempted to walk Harry and Henry. Attempted, being the operative word. Yes, for sure, it was always good old Geoff that attempted the impossible. The awesome pair could get an amazing amount of traction with their short, strong stumpy legs and I was soon to get first-hand experience, on just how much traction they could get.

In my way of thinking, TRACTION relates to the word tractor. Yes, a tractor has traction and it sure can pull, but I was soon to find out from Harry and Henry what pulling was really about. So our bright and breezy boarding kennel proprietor attempted to walk off happily into the sunset, sorry wrong word, I mean woodland, with his two new playmates!

So, here we go...

Walking along our woodland path I had only achieved a distance of about fifty yards when I learnt what Bassets are all about. Simultaneously, without any warning, they dumped their backsides down.

Why?

Because the two daft stubborn hounds decided

they just didn't want to go any further!

I tried to encourage them with a gentle pull that soon became a dragging competition. I was having absolutely no success at all. It didn't take many seconds for me to realise that I stood no chance of winning our tug-of-war contest.

For sure, these hounds were not going anywhere, anytime soon.

To my mind, the tug-of-war competition, of man against Hound was totally unfair because, after all, I only had two legs against their eight. Also, their combined weight was much, much heavier than mine. At the speed it was taking the three of us on that walk, I thought the staff would soon be sending out a search party!

But...

That was about to change!

All of a sudden, Harry let out a baleful wail, with Henry mournfully joining her a split second later.

'Oh no! Not the scent of a rabbit!'

With that, the three of us launched from nought

to sixty miles an hour in three seconds, or so it seemed.

I was being dragged like I didn't exist!

I was completely out of control, at a speed that I didn't think two lumbering Basset Hounds were capable of. The three of us were cracking along at a fair old lick with two out of three of us baying like banshees.

Me, I was getting ready to scream because...

Looming fast, out of the blue was a silver birch tree.

The tree was about twelve inches in diameter, a lovely specimen with silver bark and black blemishes reflecting in the sunshine. It had never been an intention of mine to fell one of those beautiful trees with my head or my body, but with the course I was reluctantly on, I stood a very good chance of doing so.

I had no choice but to do the unthinkable...

I let go of one of the leads.

It was Harry's!

For Christ's sake, don't tell Mother! You will know exactly what I am referring to if you have read the hilarious story of Mother in my first book.

So, off shot Harry into the undergrowth, as I desperately hung onto the other idiot.

I only just managed to avoid the oncoming birch tree as Henry and I sidestepped and careered after her sibling. Actually, it was quite an exciting journey as we charged and bulldozed our way through four-foot high bracken, nettles and knee-ripping briars. To add a bit of drama to my educational journey inspecting woodland plant life, my two protégés were baying louder than a pack of Foxhounds.

The way their sound was travelling, the locals must have thought the hunting season had started early this year! All this excitement happened before the ban on fox hunting.

It was a warm day and I was wearing shorts, I felt I had acquired enough briars and thorns in my bleeding nettle-stung knees and legs to make a wooden leg!

When we eventually caught up with Harry, I

was still hanging onto Henry's lead with her on the other end, plus what looked like a hundredweight of vegetation attached to it. My right arm was also badly scratched and into the bargain, I had been nettled there as well.

Harry and Henry never caught their rabbit, but instead, they found a rabbit hole dug under our wire netting fence designed to keep the large population of hungry plant-eating rabbits out. Well, at least that was one favour they did for me.

'I'll block that hole up later, well that's if I ever get back with these two idiots before dark!'

Eventually, I did get the two nutters back to civilisation, but with many stops, starts, drags, pulls, and of course, a few blaspheming words from me!

When I arrived back, looking like I had been lost in the jungle without a machete, my manager Pat gave me a knowing smile.

Grinning, she said,

"You seem to have been a long time Geoff?"

I just gave her a hard knowing look, realising that she had set me up!

I was absolutely certain, as a joke, she knew all about the character of Basset Hounds and relished what I was in for when I set off on my memorable walk.

Well, I suppose I deserved it, after the prank I played on her in the first book in this series about Percy a West Highland Terrier.

She always said that she would get me back.

Good one Pat!

Other staff attempted to walk the two Basset nightmares, but it was absolutely impossible, they were just so stubborn.

If they wanted to stop, they stopped!

If they wanted to go, they went!

We never had a say in the matter!

They just did as they pleased!

In the end, we found the best option was to let Harry and Henry out at lunchtime, when we were closed, letting them wander around on our large lawn. We made sure we had closed the five-bar boundary gate confining them within our grounds. Also, there was no likelihood of rabbits being around in that large lawned area. They just mooched about at their normal Basset speed, which was slower than slow, yet another reason why they were impossible to walk.

Harry and Henry came to us many, many times and we always used the same routine, but sometimes we did have a few adventures with them when they roamed our grounds.

Occasionally, the terrible twins decided to disappear. That was no problem because we knew that they couldn't get far with our grounds being fenced in. At least they couldn't climb.

But on the odd occasion, we did have to go and hunt for them.

We found them behind the cattery.

We found them behind my private dog kennels.

We found them, anywhere and everywhere that they were not meant to be!

We even found them in our private garden, two hundred yards away from the entrance to the kennel block.

One disastrous day, we found the mischievous hounds behind the cattery building looking well pleased with themselves. They were sitting proudly amongst numerous black plastic bin bags that were full of used cat litter and waste cat food. The sealed bags were always stored there until I picked them up twice a week and took them down to the large wheelie bins situated at the end of our drive. Before I could get to the job, the terrible twins had ripped the bags wide open. Obviously, with their incredible sense of smell, they had smelt the waste cat food inside, even though the bags had been completely sealed. The used cat litter consisted of wood shavings soaked in cat pee and cat crap. And of course, they had wolfed down any smelly waste cat food that they had found in the bags.

YUK!

They looked a rare sight, covered in wood shavings that they had obviously rolled in, and they stank awful too. For sure, they were certainly in need of a bath, And that's a massive understatement if ever I made one.

How on earth, could we have explained to the terrible twin's owners, why their dogs smelt of cat pee and cat crap? What would they have thought?

What a mischievous pair of characters they were.

Here is yet another little trick Harry and Henry performed.

Did I say Little?

This little trick, or more like a disaster, occurred just before our young staff were about to start the afternoon's entertainment. Meaning working with cats and dogs.

It was at the end of their lunch hour when they walked out of the staffroom onto the car park.

They were stopped in their tracks...

By a terrible vision...

The twins had been busy!

Very busy!!!

The car park was completely littered with...

Dozens and dozens of empty dog meat cans that had been licked completely clean removing the rotting remnants inside.

Yuk!!!

Unfortunately, the unstoppable siblings had found a number of rank-smelling bin bags between the staffroom and kennel block number two. The rubbish, now spread all over the car park was originally sealed in black plastic bin bags. One of the young staff members had forgotten to put them in the trailer coupled to the back of my 4 x 4 vehicle. But of course, with their amazing sense of smell, it hadn't taken our two mischievous friends long to find them.

A matter of seconds comes to mind!

The poor girl, who shall remain nameless, had made the big, big mistake of forgetting just who was going to be loosed out of the kennel block that lunchtime. So, the staff instead of getting on with their normal afternoon work, helped her with the job of picking up all the stinking rubbish.

At least they wore rubber gloves.

But unfortunately, they had no clothes pegs on their noses!

For sure, none of them ever made the same mistake again!

It certainly wouldn't have been a very good advert for our business, if our customers had seen all the stinking litter spread across our car park that day.

I was a stickler for keeping the premises scrupulously tidy, and if I saw as much as a discarded cigarette butt, I picked the horrible thing up. Thankfully, I never smoked!

I have to say we always had a good laugh about Harry and Henry's adventures.

But during the memorable events, it never seemed quite so funny!

I do have to say, despite their mischievous faults, we loved them and enjoyed having them.

Well, most of the time!

Goldie and Suzie

Once upon a time, I always wanted to write those words, we had two lovely golden Labradors boarding with us for their very first holiday. They were trained gundogs.

One was named Goldie, I am sure a lot of imagination must have gone into that name, and the other one was named Suzie. As usual for Labradors, they were very good-natured and had a habit that was not annoying at all. It was an absolute pleasure to have them staying with us and more of a pleasure to walk them.

In fact, all the staff queued up to walk the two golden girls!

So why was that you might ask?

Well, here comes the answer...

When the Lab's owner gave us his instructions on how to walk Goldie and Suzie we were highly amused.

Before I started the business it never crossed my

mind that somebody in the future would tell me, supposedly one of the best gundog trainers around, how to walk a dog. I mean what you do is, you put the dog on a lead and with the dog at your side, you place one foot in front of the other. Surely that's called dog walking!

Well, that was not the case with the owner's instructions relating to Goldie and Suzie.

He said,

"Don't put Goldie and Suzie on their leads because they just won't come with you. They like to carry their leads in their mouths when they go for a walk."

'Oh, No! I can see disaster looming up with these two beauties. I hope they don't disappear over the horizon!'

Just like Benson did in my first book!

I was not too keen, but of course, the customer is always right. Well, that's what I had to believe!

So with a bit of hesitation, we followed the owner's instructions.

And guess what, it worked.

As per usual, the customer is always right!

And this was ours, or should I say their routine...

Every walking session, we walked into Goldie and Suzie's run, holding their leads in our hands. Very gently they took them from us. Then we set off into the bordering woodland and walked along the peaty path at a leisurely pace, with the golden pair walking obediently to heel.

Amazing!

The first time I took them, I was a bit apprehensive about this new way of dog walking, but it worked very well.

There was only one slight problem...

Normally, we walked along the circular woodland path in an anti-clockwise direction. Don't ask me why, we just did. That was the direction we first started walking in and by then it was a habit. And as we all know the saying, 'Old habits die hard'. I must admit, I had never thought about it until Goldie and Suzie arrived on the scene, or should I say on the walk. But they just would not have it. They wanted to go clockwise, which was in the opposite direction to everyone else. I tried every which way, but they had to have it their way, they just insisted on going clockwise. Well, besides being taught a new way of dog walking, they also taught me in which direction I should go!

The problem we had with this new direction of dog walking was obvious, the rest of the staff with their charges, were coming from the opposite direction. As placid as the two Labs were, other dogs could be unpredictable, and occasionally, we did have the odd bully, or even psychopath boarding with us. The last thing I wanted, was to have large chunks taken out of our two golden friends. So, when the golden girls were on the circuit, we made doubly sure that the only other dogs out there had the temperament of teddy bears.

Of course, in hindsight, we could all have changed direction, perhaps that would have been much simpler, or would it have created more confusion, I am not really sure.

Wouldn't life have been so much easier for us, if all the dogs that boarded with us took themselves for a walk and were like the gorgeous golden duo?

No wonder all the staff, including myself, queued

up to walk, those golden Labradors, Goldie and Suzie!

Barclay

Barclay was a lovely-natured Bearded Collie, and he was also another of our regular guests. I never found this breed of dog to have a fantastic IQ, and Barclay certainly didn't disappoint me in that field.

He was a real puller, and that's yet another one of my understatements if I ever made one!

When Barclay was on his lead, he wore a choke chain that had no effect on him whatsoever.

BUT BOY, COULD HE PULL!

Reputedly, I was the strongest person on the premises because I was the only male, so I certainly had more than my fair share of walking the more than boisterous Barclay the pulling machine.

We found it amazing just how many of our customers had dogs that virtually ripped our arms out of our sockets.

Early one evening when Barclay was boarding with us, Kathy and I were travelling in our 4 x 4 through a nearby Shropshire village called Edgmond. Kathy pointed out to a man walking his dog.

Or was it the dog walking the man?

Kathy laughed and said,

“Who do you think is walking who?”

I started to laugh as I watched the pair striding away. The man had his arm stretched horizontally, as he marched along at an uncomfortable speed right up on his toes.

Kathy continued,

“Do you think he is enjoying his walk?”

I was not sure if she meant the man or the dog!

I could hardly reply for laughing and could only think of Barclay.

I said,

"Well, I can't say that I have a wonderful time with Barclay when he drags me along like that. I often wonder how Barclay’s owner copes with him?"

Another terrible habit Barclay had was jumping all over me when I tried to get his choke chain on. And then when I eventually lassoed him, he attempted and generally succeeded to drag me at full throttle around the wood. Perhaps he wanted to hold the record for the fastest walk!

Even when I wrenched him back off his feet, he wouldn't take any notice and immediately reverted to his own chosen speed.

And wait for it...

Just as you adjusted to his ridiculous speed, for no apparent reason at all, he did a full-blown emergency STOP and plonked himself down in a sitting position.

Guess who that reminds me of?

The two floppy-eared Basset Hounds, of course.

Barclay's unpredictable action with my added momentum took me completely by surprise and his quick manoeuvre threw me totally off-balance, creating a spectacular head-over-heels fall, in which hopefully I didn't end up in a pile of dog crap. I must add, it wouldn't have been produced by Barclay, because he saved his toiletry habits for when he returned to his run. The reason was, he had no time to go on his walk, what the dog walking session is intended for.

I think, if I had tapped Barclay on his head it

would have echoed. For sure, there must have been plenty of space inside because there was not too much inside in the way of brains!

Well, at least he was harmless, not like some of the characters I met, especially, in book one!

A Tale of two Shepherds

On yet another day of heavy English rain, two German Shepherds turned up for their first stay with us. These two dogs were totally different to Barclay, the reason being…

They had brains!

Perhaps I am a little bit unfair to Barclay because he did have a very nice temperament, he just lacked a bit of the old grey matter.

Am I repeating myself?

The rain was absolutely chucking it down in buckets when the two German Shepherds arrived, and the ground was very, very wet underfoot, in fact, it was downright sodden.

Pat and I checked the two vaccination certificates and okayed them.

Their owner Mr Jyles, a soft-spoken man said,

“They have a tendency to pull a little at times.”

‘OH, NO!!!’

Immediately, I thought of Barclay.

Forcing bravado, I replied,

“Don’t worry, Mr Jyles, we are used to dogs that pull.”

With that, Mr Jyles walked across the car park and opened the back of his blue Ford Fiesta hatchback. I have to say that I was really impressed by the obedience shown by the two Shepherds, meaning they didn't come storming out like so many other dogs did. They just sat there patiently waiting until their owner gave the order. Then with a click of his fingers, they jumped out and sat at his feet with their bushy tails thrashing away in anticipation of an exciting new adventure.

Exciting for them, but little did I realise that it was going to be quite exciting for me as well!

Mr Jyles handed me the leads with the two large Shepherds firmly attached. Then the three of us set off across the soaked grass approaching the corner of the kennel block, which was the start of our walk toward the wood. But as soon as me and my new playmates set foot on the slippery grass they started to pull.

And when I say pull.

I MEAN PULL!

I felt as if I was being pulled by a team of Huskies. Desperately, I tried to dig my heels in, but it made not the slightest bit of difference. We were moving at breakneck speed and my heels stood no chance of getting a decent purchase on the greasy surface. As all this entertainment was taking place, Mr Jyles and Pat watched in amazement as I travelled at least fifteen yards with my heels locked in the same position. I disappeared around the corner of the kennel building heading for the wood at a speed in excess of ten miles an hour and unbelievably stayed on my feet.

Looking on with amusement, Mr Jyles said,

“Your boss has got incredible balance.”

Pat laughed.

“Yes, he has. Apparently, he is quite good at skiing.”

Mr Jyles looked at my most perfect parallel skid marks.

And said,

“Hmm, yes. I can well believe it the speed he flew around that corner."

Records are there to be broken, so the saying goes, but this was one skidding record that never stood a chance of getting broken. How I managed to stay upright in that very wet wood, I will never know. The two Shepherds pulled me around the wood as if I was as light as a feather. From that day on, we always made sure that it was two of us that took those four-legged pulling machines for their walks.

Dobermans

Now we have the exciting intricacies of walking the Doberman breed.

So here we go…

Dobermans, when it was time for their walks, were just as keen to go as any other breed of dog, if not keener.

But, we found most of them had a very annoying habit!

More often than not they came in pairs and there was not a pair crazier than these two, Max and Bruce.

We nicknamed them, Mad Max and Boisterous Bruce.

You will soon find out why!

During every dog walking session, as we walked up to M. M. & B. B.'s run, they barked excitingly and reared up on their hind legs, placing their large paws on the galvanised mesh gate. All the gates to the runs opened inwards, so with their combined weight pressing against the gate, it made it very difficult to push it open and gain access. When we eventually won the battle and squeezed inside, that's when the struggle began.

Attempting to put their leads on, was an absolute...

NIGHTMARE!!!

With growing excitement and impatience they tried to push past us, or even knock us over, totally ignoring the leads in our hands in their efforts to rush out for their intended walk. And then what did the nutters do? They put their noses down, almost touching the concrete floor running round and round in tight circles in their mounting excitement to get out. These Doberman antics made it almost impossible to get their leads on.

Another frustrating habit of the Doberman breed was standing on their hind legs and pawing us on the chest. So if we had two of the idiots in there it made life very difficult for us, to say the least.

On reflection, a wrestling bout with a headlock comes to mind.

The worst problem of all was when they started to pee on you in their excitement to go for their walk.

Mind you, it was not just Dobermans that peed all over us.

Many other breeds did too!

This certainly was not my idea of having fun, especially when you had plenty of other dogs waiting to give you the same treatment.

Leads supplied by Doberman owners were usually very short, in fact only about eighteen inches long.

Whose clever idea was that?

Have you ever tried walking a big dog, or even two that pull with such a short lead?

An uncomfortable experience I can tell you.

There was no leeway with the short leads, we kept tripping over the dog that we were trying to walk, as it wove from side to side, causing us to stumble or almost fall over every few yards.

Two Dobermans together made it a double nightmare because of their sheer strength. And if they both decided to change direction rapidly, we had no alternative but to go with them. We had to hang on at a speed with arms outstretched that we hadn't contemplated. And if a pair of large Dobermans decided to go either side of a small tree, it could seriously damage your health.

Hospital visits have never been too high on my list of priorities!

So we found it much easier to use our much longer leads with choke chains on large boisterous dogs such as Dobermans. Also, it was easier to lasso them with the noose of the chain as they careered crazily inside their run. The way Dobermans performed you might think that they didn't like the choke-chain. But once we had them lassoed, they were as keen as mustard and exploded out of their run like erupting volcanos with us hanging on like 'grim death'.

At least choke-chains did control they're pulling a little and if they did pull, it was them that got short of breath, not us. Also, if they pulled backwards, the chain was virtually impossible to slip over their heads as easily as a leather collar.

So why were the majority of Dobermans like this?

I think only a Doberman could answer that question because, in our experience, they were the only breed to have these peculiar habits.

Can you imagine how long it would have

taken us, with the kennels absolutely full, to complete a walking session if all the dogs were Dobermans?

With me being a glutton for punishment, I had a crazy idea for M. M. & B. B. in the next set of stories.

Extending Leads

Customers usually supplied their own dog leads. They came in all sorts of sizes and in various conditions, and some in our opinion were totally unsuitable for their particular breed of dog. In fact, a couple of owners even came with baling twine which is normally used on farms for securing bales of straw or hay.

A very good idea for walking dogs is the extending lead. This great invention gave the dogs a lot more exercise, they were able to run around more freely. Very often, the extending leads that many customers supplied, were nowhere near strong enough for their dog. So, instead of us damaging their leads, and getting blamed for it, we used our own much stronger extenders.

Have you ever tried walking two large dogs at the same time with extending leads?

Not for the faint-hearted, I can assure you.

And I tried it on with Mad Max and Boisterous Bruce.

Arghhh!!!

Am I crazy, Or what?

Stupidly, I put the complete nutters on our extending leads and set off into the woodland.

As soon as we got on to a straight length of the path, I pressed both buttons which released the extending cords. The pair of Dobermans couldn't believe their luck and shot forward increasing their distance from me as they found their new freedom. Then for some unknown reason, only known to the Doberman breed, M. M. ran a bit further forward as B. B. ran back and passed behind me. This caught me totally by surprise. Still, I did manage to press both stop buttons simultaneously and was left standing with both arms outstretched as I took the full strain of the two idiots as they skidded to an emergency stop.

After their surprising manoeuvre, with both arms extended, I could only describe myself as being in the 'Jesus Christ' position.

I shouted at them to come back and to my surprise...

They did!

But at speed.

How incredibly obedient those two dogs were. But the problem was, they didn't stop at my feet. They careered right past me and went a similar distance before skidding to a stop as the cords became tort.

The only difference was, they had changed places. I was left with my arms folded across my chest, which was being crushed by the strength of the two dogs pulling in opposite directions.

Observing the tangled mess I had got myself into, other members of staff walking their own charges erupted with laughter. There I was, supposedly one of the most knowledgeable dog men on the planet, being made a spectacle of, by two 'doolally' Dobermans.

So what was I going to do?

Scream for help came to mind!

My arms were crushing my chest, making it difficult for me to breathe. I called the Dobermans again and once more they reacted immediately and changed positions, which returned me to the former 'Jesus Christ' position!

'ARGHHH!!!'

Were these crazy hounds having fun, or what?

Well, that was a much more comfortable position. At least I was not getting a crushed chest and I could breathe normally. And to cap it all, the wood was ringing with laughter from all my amused staff.

I shouted,

"I'm sure these dogs have done this before. They're making me look a right fool!"

I think they agreed with me and their laughter increased even more.

'I've had enough of this!'

So I pleaded,

"Can one of you please give me a hand? I'm getting nowhere with these mad idiots!"

At least one of them felt sorry for me. It was little Amy walking a frequent visitor of ours, a cute Shih Tzu named Suzie.

She walked over with Suzie who appeared to have a grin on her face, (could this be my warped imagination?) and rescued me by taking one of the extenders.

My immediate thoughts were…

'Perhaps the extending leads aren't a good invention after all!'

And here comes another fun day, did I say fun?

I was holding an extending lead in my right hand with a small black mongrel cross called Jim on the other end. For a small dog, he had a very good turn of speed. Accompanying Jim and me was a yellow Labrador called Beth, she was on an ordinary lead which was held in my left hand.

Take note, it was a nice summer's day, so I was

wearing shorts and a T-shirt.

As we walked at a fair pace, little Jim shot off forward several times, then U-turned running at full tilt toward me and Beth. I think Beth was getting a little bit jealous of Jim's freedom because, during one of Jim’s runs toward us, Beth made a playful lunge at him. Little Jim dodged and then ran right around me playing hide and seek with Beth. Unfortunately for me, the cord of the extension lead went around my bare legs, sawing into them making colourful rope burns.

It hurt like crazy and I felt like a right idiot in front of the other dog walkers.

As I was desperately trying to disentangle myself, all the girls walking their charges watched their crazy boss with their laughter ringing in my ears.

Fortunately, after that little episode, the walk carried on with no more traumas.

When I got back into the kennels, I examined my painful legs and they were both scarred bright red from the speeding cutting cord.

I looked like I had been horsewhipped!

I never seemed to learn with those extending leads, because on occasions I have had the same thing happen to my arms and I can assure you those cords cutting into your bare skin, or anywhere on your delicate body, didn't half give you a good old stinging burn.

The only consolation was, it was not always just me who suffered the cord burns, we all managed to acquire them at some time or other, no matter how careful we tried to be.

Some dogs took us completely by surprise as they sped past us and around us with the cords inflicting damage on our vulnerable bodies. The scars stayed for many months afterwards, proving just how masterful, we were not, with those extending leads.

A record I hold, never to be broken was walking five dogs at a time. It doesn't take much of a mathematician, or rocket scientist to work out that walking five dogs together, as opposed to two, meant that dog walking sessions would be accomplished in a much quicker time.

But I can assure you, none of the five were German Shepherds! No, they were five small dogs of various breeds, none of them any bigger than a small Labrador, and from my experience, I can tell you it was far from easy.

So how did I do it?

Here are the names and breeds of my five canine companions...

Jack, a Jack Russell. Two pugs, Timmy and Henry. Little Jim, the mongrel cross paired with Beth earlier. And last but not least, Herbie a lovable Border Terrier. Oh, and not forgetting the human member of the gang...

Crazy Geoff!

Jack was on an extending lead and the other four members of my gang were on standard leather leads. I held the leather leads, two in each hand and held Jack's plastic extender also in my right hand. My plan was to have two dogs on either side of me and Jack in the middle. So, with Jack released on the extender, hopefully, he would behave himself ten yards or so upfront.

Well, that was the plan.

It sounded so simple.

But was it?

So with that in mind, the gang of six set off into the beautiful woodland.

Never to be seen again?

Here comes the fun...

Jack on the extending lead, needed my greatest concentration because the little devil had serious ambitions of trying to create a world record by pulling down as many trees as he possibly could. The other four didn't exactly behave themselves either. They crossed over leads and got tangled up with each other, therefore creating absolute mayhem. Sometimes, my hands were a blur as I swapped leads from one to the other. I must say I got quite adept at walking the pack of five and certainly found it a real laugh, and certainly a challenge.

On one of those memorable walks, as I was concentrating on how to untangle Jack from a large strand of bracken, Jim took the greatest of pleasure by using me as a tree and peed down my leg. It was summer, so I was wearing shorts, and I must say, I was not too pleased with Jim's warm pee running down my leg and finally trickling into my new trainers.

The other canine prank my friend Jack did, was to run back at speed directly toward us then run behind and around us creating a real tangle. So, all the lead swapping from hand to hand started all over again.

But I am a determined ‘fella’ because I walked those five buddies on a regular basis.

The only reason I held that record of walking five dogs simultaneously was, no one else was daft enough to try it.

All the adventures I had with my gang of five created a lot of amusement for the on-looking staff.

I have to say, besides entertaining our staff, I had a lot of fun coping with my numerous adventures on those memorable walks.

But in the end, I definitely proved…

It didn’t save any time at all!

CHAPTER 5

A Chinese Take-Away

Here we have an amusing event involving a Chinese lady, but it certainly was not amusing for me. This remarkable story builds up to its unbelievable climax.

Before we started the Pet Hotel, in front of our picturesque sandstone cottage was a rough paddock. The paddock had been used for grazing by Kosha, a lovely-natured horse belonging to my wife Kathy.

I wanted to replace the paddock with a large attractive lawn that would extend from the front of our cottage, alongside the cattery right up to the kennel block and border the car park. It was going to be so big that it would be more like a small playing field. The landscaped lawn would be approximately one and a half acres in size. So, I needed someone with a tractor and plough.

My farmer friend David Craddock from next door, well, just over half a mile away, kindly offered me the use of one of his farm workers named Peter. Peter arrived, driving a massive blue Ford four-wheel drive tractor. On the back of the tractor was a plough with four gleaming blades. It certainly looked like this awesome machinery was going to murder the job at hand. And, for sure, in less than an hour the job was well-done. So, with that first job completed, Peter hurried back to the farm. Within thirty minutes, he was back with a different implement, a rotator, coupled up to the rear of the tractor. This impressive piece of machinery tore in and quickly broke up the neatly ridged soil levelling it simultaneously. The damp soil was almost black and had a lovely earthy smell. Peter did a fantastic job with David's modern machinery, and the area looked even more extensive than before.

According to local farmers, the soil in our area was some of the finest in Shropshire. For hundreds of years, it had been woodland and, therefore, naturally fertilised. The ground was ideal for growing grass or corn, and in our case, it was going to be top-quality grass.

Now it was Geoff's turn. He was going to be the one to sow the grass seed. Farmer David recommended a local seed merchant whom I contacted by phone. The seed merchant advised me which was the best type of grass needed to cope with, hopefully, hordes of future customers trampling over it on their way from the car park to inspect the cattery's accommodation. It turned out to be the same type of seed used for cricket and baseball pitches. For sure, if it was good enough for sports fields, it would be good enough for me.

Returning from the seed merchants, I unloaded two one hundred weight bags of the chosen seed from the back of my 4 x 4 vehicle. Now I was more than ready for action. I decided to tip the lawn seed into a bucket and throw it out by hand. When I was a gamekeeper I had scattered wheat corn in the same way, when I fed hundreds of pheasants as they scurried around my feet, pecking and scratching the leaf-covered woodland floor. It only took me about an hour to scatter the grass seed, which was equivalent to feeding about ten thousand pheasants. I felt more than pleased with the finished result because the seeds seemed to have scattered very evenly.

Peter returned with the tractor again, with a set of chain harrows, a bit like a giant rake, and did another excellent job of harrowing the grass seed into the rich soil.

When he had finished, he jumped down off the tractor and said,

"That's it, Geoff. All done."

"Hey Pete, don't you think we ought to roll it?"

“Only if you intend to drive vehicles on it, I am sure you haven’t intended this lovely lawn to be used as a road. Have you?”

I laughed and said,

“Over my dead body!”

Coincidentally, I found out later that his question and my statement were not so funny.

I built the car park to cope with at least twenty cars. Why on earth would anyone think of driving a vehicle across my lovely lawn? The only vehicle I intended to go on that beautiful new grass would be a brand-new ride-on-mower.

The day after I had sown the seed, we had rain all day, and it couldn’t have been better timed than if I had turned on a hosepipe. Instead of coming down in torrents, it came down steadily all day long. It soaked the grass seed good and proper, therefore naturally settling the ground as well. It was absolutely perfect growing weather.

The following day I noticed that the rain had washed many stones up to the surface as the soil had settled, and some were quite large. I decided I needed to pick them up and the only way was by hand. So, I enlisted the help of my two loyal helpers, Kathy and Ann.

With buckets in their hands, the girls picked up the offending stones, and I used a wheelbarrow to carry them off into the nearby oak wood. The stones rattled out of the barrow as I tipped them into a convenient man-made pit hole. After a rewarding but backbreaking hard day's work, there was not an offending stone insight.

I had gone to great pains to find out which would be the best ride-on-mower for the job and had narrowed it down to a streamlined Honda with an automatic gearbox or the tough Wheel Horse tractor. For almost a week, I had shopped around on the phone after thumbing through Yellow Pages. A dealer-owner with a firm from Craven Arms had given me the best price. The dealer, Mr Griffiths, had the dealership for both Honda and Wheel Horse.

I drove the very scenic route leading to Craven Arms from one side of Shropshire to the other. Just over an hour later I arrived at Mr Griffith's premises and met him outside a large red brick building. It was a garage and showroom for garden tractors. We greeted each other, shook hands, and I followed him inside the showroom, where there were miniature tractors of all shapes and sizes. I admired the new Honda and Wheel

Horse tractors on display and had great difficulty making a decision.

He walked me over to another part of the building and showed me an old red Wheel Horse tractor and said,

"How old do you think this machine is?

I replied,

"About seven years."

"Geoff, you are a little bit out. It's twenty-three years old, and it's in for its annual service."

I was gob-smacked!

Instantly, I decided it had to be a new Wheel Horse. The price was four thousand six hundred pounds, it was a lot more money than I had intended to spend, but I wanted that brand spanking new red tractor. As luck would have it, winter was approaching fast, and Mr Griffiths wanted to get rid of some stock. After a conversation, almost like bidding at an auction, I ended up with a bargain and only paid three thousand eight hundred pounds.

Before we shook hands and struck the deal, Mr

Griffiths cracked a joke and said,

"If you had carried on haggling, I would have offered you twenty quid just to go away."

Actually, his words were a bit stronger than that!

I just couldn't wait for my red tractor to be delivered. We all know every little boy's dream is to own a red tractor. I was fortunate enough to have a toy one when I was a little boy, but my new one was going to be a lot bigger.

The gleaming red tractor mower was delivered at the end of September on the back of a light lorry by Mr Griffiths personally. After unloading the gleaming machine, he explained all the controls to me. It had a forty-two-inch rotary cut with a high and a low ratio gearbox, making eight gears in all. It was so powerful its front wheels would do a wheelie if you let the clutch out too quickly. It was like having an expensive toy. In fact, it was an expensive toy, and I knew from that day I was going to have many enjoyable hours sitting on my lovely red tractor.

That evening Kathy, her sister Ann, and my Mum decided they would like to try out my new toy. Anyone would think it was a Ferrari. At least it was red! In great detail, I explained to them that they needed to release the clutch very slowly. But did they listen? Did they heck?

The two sisters and Mum in turn started off on the tarmacadam drive at the front of our cottage heading for the car park in front of the brand-new kennel block building. All three of them performed unexpected great big wheelies and squealed with fright as the front wheels lifted off the driveway. Once the wheels touched back down on terra-firma, they all had beaming faces as they drove with growing confidence. Little did they know it would be their first and last ride on **MY** tractor.

The three joyriders

It usually takes around ten days for new grass

shoots to appear, and three weeks after their emergence, the delicate grass would be ready for its very first light cut. I was so excited and desperate to use my new toy. I even contemplated cutting some long grass on the neighbouring woodland rides. Immediately, I shelved that idea and realised I just had to be patient and wait for nature to take its course.

The grass came up right on schedule and three weeks later, as planned, I was able to give my new lawn a light top cut and, wow, give my brand-new red tractor a real workout. After completing my exciting task, I sat on the little tractor admiring how green and lush the freshly cut grass looked and how it set off the grounds so beautifully.

A fond recollection of mine is about one of my favourite birds, the swallow. As I rode the tractor cutting the grass, numerous swallows flew past hawking and hunting the flying insects that the tractor had disturbed. At times they were so close that I felt I could almost touch them as they skimmed incredibly low over the freshly cut grass almost brushing it with their long narrow, streamlined wings. The sun shone on their backs, and their glossy dark blue feathers glinted in the sun's rays. What a beautiful memory! So, whenever I smell freshly cut grass, it always conjures up that memory of those halcyon days with those graceful jet-like birds, my swallows.

How streamlined is that?

Sometimes on hot sunny days when I was mowing the large lawn, I was so relaxed and subdued with the warmth of the sun on my back and my surrounding environment, I briefly nodded off. You could always tell when that had happened because my regular, precise straight lines had the occasional large kink in them.

What on earth has this exceedingly hard work creating a vast beautiful lawn, got to do with the title of this story.

'A Chinese Take-Away'?

Well, here comes the answer.

One afternoon, I was sitting in my office next to the kennel block taking care of some paperwork when a car drove onto the car park. It was a smart red Mini Cooper S, and out stepped an attractive Asian lady, whom I presumed to be Chinese.

She walked into my office, I politely stood up, introduced myself and asked,

"How can I help you?"

She gave me a pleasant smile and said,

"Would it be possible for me to view your cattery, please? I am going away for three weeks and need to board my two cats."

I returned her smile and said,

"Ok, no problem. If you would like to follow me down to the cattery, I'll show you around."

She followed me out of the office and I assumed she was walking right behind me. The distance across my lovely new lawn from the office to the cattery building was well over a hundred yards. I was about halfway across when I realised, I must have been walking a little too quickly because I couldn't hear her following me. So, I stopped and turned around and...

'Jesus Christ!'

Oh, she was following me all right, in fact, thirty yards behind me. To my absolute astonishment, she was in her Mini, not a mini skirt but her red Mini car!

I could not comprehend what I was seeing. The Chinese lady was driving her car, right across my newly seeded lawn!

'ARRRGH!!!'

Why hadn't I heard her car door shut?

Why hadn't I heard her car engine start?

Why hadn't I heard her car behind me?

OH, NO, my poor lovely grass. I was jumping up and down, with my hands raised above my head, making all sorts of gesticulations.

I screamed at the top of my voice,

"STOP! STOP! PLEASE GO BACK!"

My thoughts indeed contained much stronger words.

It finally dawned on her that she shouldn't have been on my lovely new lawn. So, guess what she did next?

She went back, all right. But instead of slowly reversing precisely along the same tracks she had just carved; she floored the accelerator and took off making a U-turn at a speed resembling a Monte Carlo rally driver. She spun the steering wheel to the right, hurtling back towards the car park with the little Mini's front wheels spinning and my tender grass shoots spraying out everywhere. Even a person with bad eyesight couldn't fail to notice that she had made a tremendous slick brown U-turn, damaging yet more of my lovely grass.

I walked back toward the car park with my hands in my pockets, to say the least, feeling somewhat dejected and at the same time, with my head bowed, inspecting my mangled, bruised grass. I was thinking of all the hard work we had done and how it had been a complete waste of time.

My Chinese friend apologised profusely,

"I am so sorry!"

In the traumatic, tragic circumstance in which I found myself, I smiled at her and said through gritted teeth in the most pleasant tone I struggled to muster,

"Oh, don't worry. It's no problem. It will soon grow again."

ARRRRRGH!!!

As we all know or are led to believe, the customer is always right, and I didn't want to lose a new one by showing any anger. Even though strangling her crossed my mind at the time! The good news was she loved the cattery and booked two cats in for a three-and-a-half-week stay.

Fortunately, because the car was only a Mini, it hadn't sunk into the lawn too much, and most of the damage turned out to be blackened bruised grass, very similar to frost burn. So luckily, there was no long-term damage inflicted. It was not too long before I saw the funny side of the episode. So, over the years, recalling her story to friends over dinner, we have had many a laugh over that little Chinese incident.

I am sure you can guess what sign I placed on my lovely lawn for all to see.

CHINESE PLEASE KEEP OFF THE GRASS

Well, minus the 'Chinese' part.

So, with a little bit of luck, perhaps that sign would STOP any more of those...

Chinese Mini Take-Aways.

CHAPTER 6

Get me out of here Quick!

Poppy

We had a lovely dog called Poppy staying with us on a regular basis. Now the statement 'regular basis' is a gross understatement!

Poppy was a beautiful purebred Welsh Border Collie, which is the breed that farmers use for herding sheep, also, they are used for search and rescue and are very good at it as well, with bags of energy.

Poppy was quite small with a white blaze down her face, a white chest and belly, the remainder of her was a sleek glossy black. Her ears stood up sharp like a fox and she always seemed to have a grin on her face. According to her owners Mr and Mrs Clarke she loved being with us more than being at home.

I was not surprised. She virtually lived with us.

Often the Clarkes were away from home for only half a day, if so, Poppy came to us, which meant her being dropped off at 8 am and picked up just before we closed at 5 pm. I suppose she was so happy with us because she had no canine friends at home and she didn't like to be left alone. Well, she most certainly had plenty of canine friends to choose from when she was with us.

When it was time for Poppy to leave our

premises, her owners who loved her dearly, had to virtually drag her to the car. Obviously, she did not want to leave her woodland walks and canine pals behind.

But the worst problem was when her owners were dropping her off. Poppy knew exactly where she was and where she was going and as soon as their car approached the entrance to our drive...

Poppy went ballistic!

In her mounting excitement to get out, Poppy jumped about inside the car frantically yowling her head off. In preparation for her explosive exit, she was already attached to her extending lead. As soon as the car stopped, she exploded out in a bid to get to her walk in the woods, dragging Mr or Mrs Clarke with her. Once her extension lead was released, she raced around the side of the kennel block without even waiting for one of the girls to take her.

After putting up with the intolerable sound of Poppy's barking, the beleaguered couple looked completely stressed out.

On one occasion Mrs Clarke said,

"I'm sure you must think we don't look after Poppy properly. She is fine when she's at home, but as soon as she knows she is coming here, she just goes crazy with excitement."

After dozens of visits with the yowling Poppy, her owners just couldn't stand her performances any longer. So they came up with an idea...

They decided that the only solution was to get Poppy out of the car as quickly as possible. In other words, as soon as it turned into our drive!

If there was only one of the couple (usually Mrs Clarke) delivering the energetic Border Collie, the car was parked at the bottom of our drive. The rest of their journey was completed on foot with Poppy dragging her hapless owner along our quarter-mile drive in her manic effort to get to our premises.

If the couple delivered Poppy, Mrs Clarke drove the car as Mr Clarke (what a gentleman) was dragged along the drive.

Poppy was a tremendous advert for our business and if we had ever advertised on TV, I would not have hesitated in sending a camera crew down our drive to film one of those exciting Poppy occasions!

Pip and Sam

As I am sure you have picked up, we had many dogs staying with us on an extremely regular basis. Two I remember well were Pip and Sam. They were also Border Collies and surprise, surprise, full of endless energy, which depicts the breed.

Pip and Sam had a similar habit to Poppy, they just could not wait to get out of the vehicle. In this case, it was my 4 x 4. The amazing difference was, these two head-bangers could not wait to get out because they wanted to visit the vet.

What, the vets!

Can you believe that?

Were they crazy, or what?

Now, that has got to be a rare case of canine madness, if ever there was one.

Most dogs had to be dragged to the veterinary

surgery, but not these two nutters. They dragged me in so fast my feet hardly touched the ground. I found it hard to understand why even one of those mad pair behaved in that strange way, not alone, both of them.

The mind boggles!

Perhaps it was because their owners used the same vets as us, I just don't know. But what I do know is, those two frequently had something wrong with them. I always seemed to be taking them down to the surgery and as soon as I pulled into the vets' car park, they started yowling with excitement. I have heard of people being hypochondriacs, a few friends do come to mind, but not two dogs belonging to the same family!

This definitely would not have been a good advert on TV to promote our business.

Viewers might have believed that it was our fault the two Border Collies needed to visit the vets on such a regular basis!

CHAPTER 7

Raging Bulls!

The totally different temperaments of Bull Terriers.

Yes, we boarded Bull Terriers, but we never boarded Bulls, as in the bovine variety.

However, we did have a mini invasion of cattle.

One rememberable day, after taking care of cats and dogs. Kathy and I chatted away as we walked down to the cottage readying ourselves for our evening meal. We went through our garden gate, rounded the front corner of our cottage, and lo and behold, to our horror, there was a small herd of young heifers and bullocks, (young female cows and castrated male bulls) roaming and chomping away at the plants and shrubs in the garden.

Our neighbouring farmer had not fenced them in properly.

ARGHHH!!!

This tragic mistake had allowed the small herd to escape and seriously vandalise our garden.

The cattle were from the twenty-acre field which bordered the back of our once beautiful garden. They had trampled through a barbed wire fence and easily pushed through my young beech hedge. They probably found our young plants and flowers to be a great delicacy for their evening meal, as opposed to boring grass.

Well, folks, that's all the fun of living in the countryside!

At least the sympathetic farmer paid for the damage, but it took a long time for our lovely lawn to recover, especially with deep cloven hoof prints everywhere.

Now, on the other hand, we did have quite a few 'Bull' Terriers staying with us of all shapes and sizes. But none with horns!

Bull Terrier Facts

The modern Bull Terrier descended from a cross between the Bulldog and the White English Terrier and was bred for dog fighting in the 19th century. Birmingham breeder James Hinks is credited with stabilising the breed with the addition of new blood. Some suggest the introduction of Collie blood to give the length of muzzle and the Dalmatian might also have contributed. Whilst many of the earlier examples were white, in the 1920's coloured Bull Terriers became more frequently seen and these were valuable in the breeding programme as deafness in the all-white dogs had become a problem.

On the list of canine 'Bulls', there are six distinct breeds descended from the Bull and Terrier hybrids, five of which were recognised by the American Kennel Club (AKC) in the following order. Bull Terrier, Boston Terrier, American Staffordshire Terrier, Staffordshire Bull Terrier, and Miniature Bull Terrier. And of course there is the White English Bull Terrier.

In all our years of experience, we never had any 'Raging' Bull Terriers.

But, we did have some very close calls.

Or should I say I did!

Also, I must add, that we did have some very lovable moments with the Bull Terrier breed.

Our most frequent visitors in the 'Bull' family were the Staffordshire Bull Terriers. They have a wide-grinning happy-looking face and they come in all sorts of colours, consisting of black, brown, brindle and many other mixtures. We only had a few of the all-white English Bull Terriers with their pointed snout, which I thought was a little similar to a pig's snout, but not so squashed. But we never had any Dalmatian Bull Terriers, they just have the same similar colours but where the coats are white they have black blemishes making them look similar in colour to a Dalmatian.

Maybe it was fortunate that we never had a visit from an American Bully, especially with the breed having such a bad reputation. They are making the news headlines far too frequently for my liking by attacking and killing children, adults, and even their misguided owners. So we were quite relieved that we were never asked to board a Bully because I was not sure what my response would have been.

Thinking about it, my answer would be no!

During the school holidays, we had many schoolchildren helping with dog walking, which I must say they thoroughly enjoyed, and I could never have dared put them at risk.

Albert

The English Bull Terrier with their white face, pink piggy eyes and long piggy nose, in my opinion always seemed to look aggressive and ready for a fight.

Indeed, that is what they were bred for in years gone by.

But in this day and age, nothing could be further from the truth!

They say you can't go by looks, and what a true statement that proved to be with this breed of dog.

And it was most certainly true when it came to young Albert. Yes, he was one of the white piggy breeds and for sure you could never have met a dog more lovable than our Albert. He was an expensive pure pedigree with excellent papers and his owners were very proud of him.

Albert loved to sunbathe. He had a very amusing habit of lying on the concrete floor keeled over on his side with his paws pressed against the wall of his run. To make him more comfortable we found an old wooden sunbed and put it in his kennel and as you can see, he loved it. It didn't matter how noisy the other dogs in the same kennel block were because Albert was completely oblivious and would lie in this prone position fast asleep for hours at a time.

I felt like offering him some sun cream for his unblemished white coat. I suspect he never got too hot because I am sure his white coat reflected the sun, which streamed through the corrugated fibreglass roof of his run.

I have never seen another dog of any breed lie in that tranquil position before, or since.

I took many photographs of Albert, to show his owners just how happy he was, like a contented baby. Also, I showed Albert's photos to disbelieving friends and prospective customers regarding just how much our canine guests enjoyed boarding with us. Apparently, Albert never lay in this prone position at home, this little trick was solely for our benefit.

I decided to put a notice board in the office, so I could display photographs of pets staying with us and the many letters of thanks we received from our happy customers. The photo of Albert, lying with his legs in the air sunbathing, was the most famous one. It made many of our present customers laugh and it also built up prospective customer's confidence to board their pets with us.

What a great advert Albert's photos were.

One gentleman, after seeing Albert's photo even suggested staying with him, as he believed he would have a more relaxing time with Albert, than on holiday with his wife and children.

Obviously, his wife was not with him when he made that statement!

You could just imagine them both lying there, one with a beer in his hand and maybe the other with a bone in his paw.

Albert loved to be gently rubbed and scratched on his forehead, right down to the long pointed shiny black tip of his nose. The more you scratched the harder he pushed against you, just like a cat does when you stroke it.

If every dog had been like Albert, it would have made running our boarding kennels even more enjoyable.

I have to say, Albert was one of the most placid gentlemanly dogs I was so very fortunate to meet. I regard myself to be very lucky and really appreciate having known Albert, who stayed with us many times over the years.

Blue

Then there was Blue...

Blue was a different kettle of fish compared to our ultra-placid Albert!

Blue was a jet-black Staffordshire Bull Terrier and he wore a thick brown leather collar, with short blunt brass spikes on it. Lots of Bull Terriers came to us wearing this type of collar.

I am not sure why dog owners used macho collars like that on their beloved pets, but it surely made the dogs look more aggressive, even if they were as gentle as lambs. Maybe it served as a warning to other dogs or even the general public.

I certainly didn't think it did the breed of Staffordshire Bull Terrier any favours at all.

But this Staffordshire Bull Terrier Blue was definitely one of the more macho varieties.

I can most certainly attest to that one!

Blue's collar certainly didn't do him any favours

at all. And I was about to find out why!

Any dog that arrived on our premises and looked potentially dangerous was always walked by, guess who? Well, good old Geoff of course! So I walked Blue many times and the more I walked him the more anxious I became of losing my hand, or even my arm! He had an alarming frightening habit of climbing up his lead.

Oh no, not with his front paws…

BUT WITH HIS TEETH!!!

And I can tell you his large, yellow pointed teeth looked very sharp indeed.

Blue never tried to bite my legs, so he never appeared to be dangerous in that region. Well, at least that was something to be thankful for!

As Blue walked along the woodland path with me in an unconcerned manner, right out of the blue, (I am sure that is a pun!) to my consternation, he jumped up and grabbed the slack in his leather lead and hung onto it like a crocodile. The trick for me was to try and stop his powerful set of bone-crunching gnashers from chomping their way up his lead, then eventually my juicy hand which was getting closer and closer by the second to his sharp yellow teeth.

'Jesus Christ! My arm is going to disappear down this nutter's throat up to my armpit in a minute!!!'

It didn't take many walks with Blue for me to realise that I had to keep his lead vertical and as tight as possible. I could not allow him to grab any of the slack. I just had to keep those ultra-strong jaws as far away as possible from my juicy hand. But Blue was very adept with his little party trick and no matter how careful I was, he always seemed to manage to reel most of the lead in across his powerful jaws. It got to the stage where I was walking him all the way around the wood on his hind legs with my hand held high to keep it out of reach of his chomping powerful gnashers.

A frightening scene from the movie Jaws came to mind!

One afternoon, I was losing my battle with Jaws, sorry I mean Blue, with his teeth getting uncomfortably close to my delicate hand by the second. I was taking most of his weight because the only part of him that touched the ground was the tips of his paws. In other words, he was hanging in the air almost completely off the ground. Unsurprisingly, he was getting heavier by the second. And I was tiring by the second! Well, I hung on for as long as I could and then I did the unthinkable cardinal sin that I had preached and brainwashed to all my staff and my mother in the first book...

I LET GO OF HIS LEAD!

And dropped him.

I had no choice because I was visualising that Blue's next bite was going to go right through my fingers, and for sure, I cared more about my fingers than losing the nutter on the other end.

To my surprise...

Blue ignored my hand.

And the rest of my body.

He ran off!

As fast as his short stubby legs could carry him.

I must have been feeling very brave that day because as much as I wanted to, I didn't run away in the opposite direction, but ran immediately after him. I am not sure if it was my bravery or just sheer foolhardiness that made me give chase. Anyway, I was close to his tail as I sprinted in hot pursuit after the crafty little devil. This was obviously Blue's ruse to escape, the aggressive-looking character must have been planning it all the time. He was running as fast as a Staffordshire Bull Terrier could run, which in canine terms was nowhere near the league of the dogs you see on TV, meaning greyhounds that punters place bets on, as they run after a stuffed hare.

As I legged it over bracken, briars and stinging nettles, I was gaining speed on Blue. He didn't know it, but he was heading straight for the rabbit netting that enclosed our woodland. His little piggy eyes didn't pick out the almost invisible wire mesh. To my amusement, he bulldozed the mesh at full Staffy tilt. To Blue's complete surprise, as his head hit the mesh, he rebounded slightly dazed, straight into my waiting arms.

Catching him was just pure instinct and it never crossed my mind that he could have badly bitten me.

I grabbed Blue's lead and marched him back to his quarters and he made no attempt whatsoever to grab it again. I wondered if he would try his little party trick the next time we attempted to walk together.

For sure, that was one walk I was not looking forward to.

When I took Blue out the very next morning, he didn't make any attempt to grab his lead or my hand. In fact, he never tried it again.

That was most certainly a blessing in disguise.

Blue came only one time, thank goodness. I knew his owners were exceptionally pleased when they collected him. They did question if he had been ok with us. (Hmm, I wonder why?) Of course, I kept yet another secret. I never told them about his frenzied lead chomping or our little chase around the woodland. Perhaps they had moved away from the area and next time, maybe he would try it on again at another boarding kennel.

And the best of British luck to them!

That is almost all of my stories about 'Raging Bulls'. I certainly thought Blue was on the verge of being one. Especially when his teeth were so close to my delicate pink delicious fingers!!!

Queenie

This story is about a lovely-natured little dog, that was a Staffordshire Bull Terrier in drag!

Queenie was a Staffordshire Bull Terrier, but most definitely not a Raging Bull. In fact, she was totally the opposite, she was gorgeous and her temperament was incredibly lovable. In fact, anybody would be hard-pressed to find a more lovable dog than our Queenie!

Queenie was quite small compared to most Staffy's. Her colour was a lovely tawny brown.

Because of her diminutive size, it made her head, which was the usual size for a Staffy, look even bigger. Her mouth looked as if it virtually stretched from ear to ear, resembling a giant bullfrog and she always seemed to have a permanent smile on it.

Queenie looked like a big mobile smile on little stumpy legs. Her eyes were light brown, a similar colour to her coat and her eyes always looked contented and happy. When you looked at her, she wagged her stumpy docked tail, which made the complete back end of her body shake.

Because of Queenie's lovely temperament, she was more than popular with all our staff and they literally queued up to walk her. She came to stay almost every weekend because her owner was a single lady who was going through some sort of change in her life. Hence Queenie virtually lived with us.

One day, Queenie's owner informed us that her circumstances had changed and she needed to find a home for Queenie. Well, that home didn't take too long to find. In fact, it only took a few seconds because Pat, our manager, loved Queenie to bits and jumped at the chance of taking her under her wing.

The bonus for us was Queenie often came to work with Pat, so thankfully we still saw her on a regular basis.

There you are, how about that for a nice little story about a happy little dog that wouldn't harm a fly.

So much for vicious 'Raging' Bull Terriers.

Now it is time for a cat and mole story.

CHAPTER 8

A Cat Called Mouse

This is a very special story!

We had been running the cattery and kennels for a couple of years when this story took place. It is about a cat that became very special to me, and of course, Kathy.

The girls in the cattery had informed me that they had seen a half-grown stray cat on several occasions. Kathy and I had also glimpsed the cat wandering around in the evenings, especially in our garden. The stray cat was an amazing colour. I can only describe it as being an attractive lemon-coloured tabby. It appeared to be very shy and nervous because when it was spotted, it quickly disappeared into the surrounding woodland. I was quite concerned about the stray, especially with it not being vaccinated and roaming about right outside our cattery entrance. We were all worried that the new visitor could have been carrying something contagious which could have been a major risk to our feline guests inside the cattery.

Feral cats roaming in the countryside are classed very high on the vermin list by gamekeepers, second to foxes. As I have mentioned before, I am an ex-gamekeeper. Unfortunately, on many occasions in the past, I know this sounds awful, I have had to cull feral cats, even though I have always been a fond lover of cats having grown up with one.

A feral cat is a domestic cat that has gone wild, probably because it has been dumped by its so-called caring owner. I never, ever thought that once I had finished with the game-keeping side of my working life, I would ever have to cull another cat again.

Nor did I want to!

But the question was...

Is this stray cat a danger to our guests residing in our plush cattery?

Perhaps I was going to have no alternative but to cull it.

In other words, shoot it!

I most certainly was not looking forward to that!

Ken, Kathy's brother and his wife Rosemarie were staying with us for the weekend, as they often did. Before we employed any staff, when they were over, they helped with the dog walking in the late afternoon session. Afterwards, we had fun around the dining table over dinner.

Ken often used to stand and look out at our amazing view from the dining room through the patio window. He could never sit still for too long. And still can't!

It was early evening when Ken shouted and pointed,

"HEY GEOFF, there's a molehill appearing on your lawn. Over there, look."

A mole doing what it does best

Ken knew moles were my arch enemy and I was always trying to control them, especially when they were ruining my lovely lawn. As cute as moles are, unfortunately, they can be serious pests when they tunnel under tendered lawns or even a prestigious golf course.

Moles are incredibly powerful animals and considering they are so small, within minutes of arriving in a garden, they burrow underneath the lawn, humping up the soil into quite a sizeable mound. Hence the name, molehills.

Mole catchers control moles by using metal scissor traps or poisoning them with strychnine. For sure, a terribly cruel death.

I had a much better idea. I controlled moles with a twelve-bore double-barrelled shotgun!

I know that sounds awful, but I am absolutely certain that my method was by far the most humane with it being an instantaneous death.

I rushed over to the window where Ken was standing and indeed saw that the mole was humping up a new mound of soil. I knew 'Moley' would be fairly close to the surface, so I hastily went to my gun cabinet, unlocked it, grabbed my shotgun and slipped two cartridges into the twin chambers.

With the loaded shotgun at the ready, I crept across the lawn very carefully. A mole's hearing and sense of smell are amazing, so my feet vibrating through the ground would send shockwaves alerting them of danger. So, I had to tread very lightly. It was also very important that my scent was not blown by the wind to their sensitive nostrils. Therefore, I always approached the rising mound with the wind in my face making it impossible for the busy mole to get my scent.

It was often frustratingly guaranteed, that when I had eventually crept up to the mound of moving soil, the mole underneath stopped immediately. It was amazing how the mole could somehow sense I was standing above it, no matter how careful I had been. I have often stood over a new mound of soil for as long as thirty minutes and ended the scenario by walking away in frustration knowing that the mole had gone. And for sure, it would be back again in the very near future, creating even more mini-mountains of havoc.

Anyway, on that particular day, I was to win the battle. Ken followed me every step of the way and stood a few paces behind. He wanted to witness this new way of ridding moles from lawns. As I was aiming the shotgun at the new mound of soil with the end of the twin barrels only a foot away.

The soil moved...

BANG!!!

The shotgun created a smoking hole two inches in diameter.

For sure, the mole never felt a thing.

Very often, even if the mole was completely missed, it is the massive shockwave that kills it. The fact is, a twelve bore from such a short range produces pressure in excess of one ton per square inch.

All of a sudden...

Ken grabbed my arm.

He shouted,

"QUICK GEOFF, there's that stray cat you told me about."

“SHOOT IT!"

I spun round to see the lemon tabby crossing the lawn at breakneck speed only twenty yards away. Instinctively, I released the safety catch and threw the gun into my right shoulder knowing that the second barrel was still loaded. For my ability, it was a very easy shot and I knew that the cat would be bowled over in a cartwheeling spin and killed instantly.

Swinging the barrels through the crossing target, I gave it a little lead and...

I COULD NOT DO IT!!!

I never pulled the trigger and let the little cat go.

Ken shouted,

"GEOFF! What are you playing at? Why didn't you shoot it?"

I retaliated,

"I just couldn't do it Ken!"

Amazed, Ken replied,

"You're going soft in the head, you are. What about it spreading disease around your cattery?

You won't half regret it. You told me you were going to shoot it if you saw it again."

Ken was reeling out all the things that made common sense, but in that split second when I had the fleeting opportunity, I just couldn't bring myself to pull the trigger.

At that moment, it would have been nice to have known...

It was one of the best decisions I made in my life.

So, the pretty lemon tabby survived and made its escape, and definitely used up one of its nine lives.

After the little cat's narrow escape from the 'Grim Reaper', meaning me, the girls from the cattery saw a lot more of it. Obviously, it was becoming less nervous, or perhaps it was becoming hungrier. So, with a softening heart, I instructed the girls to leave food out for the pretty stranger in a place well away from the cattery entrance. So, they did and left a dish of water and cat biscuits twenty yards away in front of our garage. And it didn't take the little stray cat long to find it and wolf it down.

In the evenings, we watched the newcomer

feeding from a discreet distance. The poor little thing was ravenous and as soon as it had eaten its food, it slinked off into the sanctuary of the bordering woodland.

As the days passed by, the little cat didn't hurry away after it had eaten its food. Slowly it became much more approachable. The girls tried to get near to it, but each time they got too close for comfort, it slinked away and disappeared.

I seem to have an affinity with animals, so I decided I would have a go at approaching the little cat.

And possibly catch it!

One evening when the cattery girls had gone home, I watched the new cat on the block eating its food. Kathy and her sister Ann were looking on from further away. I crept stealthily towards it and was about fifteen yards away when the little cat stopped eating and looked straight at me. I stopped moving and remained completely motionless. I waited until the cat started to eat again, and then moved even closer, eventually cutting the distance down to about three yards.

The cat glanced up again for a couple of seconds, showing no apparent concern, and then continued eating. I was getting quite excited and was sure I could hear my heart thumping. Again, I edged very slowly toward the cat, I was only a yard away before it stopped eating and looked directly into my eyes. Yet again, I waited until the cat resumed eating and then crouching down low, I edged nearer. When I was within touching distance, I slowly reached out to stroke its back. As I touched it, the fur shivered. Hurriedly, it carried on eating.

I stroked the little cats back once, twice, three times and amazingly it started purring. The cat finished its food as I continued stroking it. I wondered if I could pick it up, so I stroked its head and it started to purr even louder. With a quick motion, I smoothly scooped the little cat gently into my arms and held it close in a loving cuddle. Unbelievably, it never attempted to struggle and as it lay in my arms, I noticed that it was a tomcat, So, that is how I tamed the little lemon tabby and I decided from that very moment to call him Mouse. He was so small and as gentle as a mouse, as he lay in my arms contentedly purring away.

Kathy and Ann looked on in amazement as I easily performed the act of picking Mouse up. They couldn't wait to make their way over to me and give him numerous strokes, and he absolutely loved it.

It dawned on me that Mouse must have been an abandoned cat. He looked to be about four months old and was probably a Christmas kitten. It was coming up to Easter, so someone had decided that they did not want their little Christmas kitten anymore and callously abandoned him on the verge of the busy A41 highway, underneath the Cattery & Kennel sign at the end of our drive, without even worrying that he could get run over. Whoever it was, probably thought that maybe we would look after it. Little would they have known I very nearly shot the poor little thing! So, we decided there and then we would personally adopt the little stray cat. He would be the first cat I had owned since I was a boy.

This is a more explicit description of Mouse...

Mouse was a male cat with beautiful markings. His colour was predominately lemony yellow with a slightly darker gingerish colour showing through in a tabby pattern. He had a very small head and a much shorter tail than usual. His gorgeous eyes were yellow like the pale flames of a fire and he had a tiny triangular pink nose. He was incredibly vocal, in fact, he turned out to be a right noisy little devil and because of that, I would say he had Siamese in his blood. From my first-hand experience, Siamese always seem to be a very vocal breed. He also looked to have Burmese and obviously tabby because of his stripes. A right little mongrel indeed, but it certainly made him incredibly unique. I didn't realise just how lucky we were going to be in meeting Mr Mouse. In fact, we have never seen a cat that colour before or since, which made him even more unique and special.

Mouse

I knew the welcome stranger would be infested with fleas because he had been living in the woodland for weeks and I am sure that he must have come into contact with a rabbit or two. Or lived in a rabbit burrow.

And rabbits are riddled with the minute shiny brown parasites!

That evening, because of the flea problem, Kathy and I decided to allow Mouse to sleep in our utility room. In fact, later on in Mouse's story, the utility became his permanent bedroom.

Within twenty-four hours of Mouse entering our home or should I say the utility, we zapped him with flea spray and had him vaccinated the following day.

No way, did I want an unvaccinated cat on the premises. Thank you very much!

The vet confirmed that Mouse was a very healthy cat, and probably between four and five months old. The little lad gave the vet no trouble at all as he examined him and vaccinated him. Also, he commented on Mouse's beautiful rare colour. With the vet's kind words, I noticed that Kathy's eyes lit up as she felt so proud of her new baby boy.

Mouse needed to be neutered and the operation is usually performed when cats are around six months old. The vet suggested we brought him back down to the surgery in about four weeks, to get the chop.

The dreaded day soon came around and we took Mousey down to the veterinary practice to have the little lad neutered. If only he had known what was in store for him, I am sure he would have given some resistance.

I know I would!

After his operation, Mouse returned home the same evening very, very subdued, and who could blame him? He was still under the effect of the anaesthetic, but he still kept trying to walk and just kept toppling over. It was so funny to watch him because he appeared to be so drunk, but we did feel very sorry for him.

Especially me!

As they say, time is a great healer and within a few days Mouse was none the worse for wear after his horrible ordeal, and at least he could look forward to his new life with us. Hopefully, there wouldn't be any horrible operations for him in the future. For sure, Mouse's life would certainly be a lot better than living in the wild, fending for himself in all types of inclement weather and with no proper shelter.

Mouse quickly got very attached to us, and when we took our own dogs for a walk in the evenings, he followed us. It was a lovely sight to see three Springer Spaniels running around with a cat following behind. We always started our walk in the twenty-acre grass field behind our cottage and the prairie-sized field was sparsely dotted with a number of old oak trees.

When Mouse joined us on these walks, he seemed to be quite nervous and stopped in the shadow of the first oak tree's shadow offering protection from above and then as we approached the next one, he ran full pelt across the open ground to join us. I put this strange behaviour down to his feline instinct. He obviously felt vulnerable being out in the open and his instinct was telling him to get under cover, probably thinking that he could be open to an attack from above by a large bird of prey, such as an eagle or buzzard. He wasn't to know at that time that the only eagles that lived in the British Isles were the golden variety. They only reside in Scotland and the likelihood of a buzzard attacking him that were quite common in our area, was pretty remote because they prefer carrion, in other words, the decaying flesh of dead animals.

Here is a little bit of Geoff's knowledge about nature...

Eagle Fact

The magnificent golden eagle was the largest bird of prey in the UK with a wingspan of seven feet eight inches. In recent years, displacing the golden eagle is the white-tailed eagle, also known as the sea eagle. It has an eight feet wingspan and preys on fish, mammals and small birds. It was persecuted to extinction in the UK, but sixty were reintroduced from Norway during the 1970s after an absence of 243 years. Today, around forty pairs now nest in Scotland. In 2019 twelve white-tailed eagles were released on the Isle of White. As I am writing this in July 2023, the hot news is a twelve-week-old white-tailed eagle chick has fledged the nest and is being taken care of by the parents.

What a brilliant conservation story that is!

A white-tailed sea eagle in action

Well, after that informative bit of information, it's back to Mouse...

Mouse always made sure that he never lost sight of his new home that he had quickly grown to love. So once out of his comfort zone, he quickly made his way back to our cottage flitting from oak tree to oak tree. We carried on with the walk with the Springers and when we eventually arrived back, he was there to greet us with some very loud meowing in his relief to see us arriving back safely.

Mouse had previously survived in the wild, so his old habits had remained with him. Sadly, he was an expert killer!

The only good thing that pleased Kathy was, he rarely ate his prey, probably because he was being fed so well. He hunted every waking hour, although like most cats he got his fair share of sleep. For the local wildlife, that must have been a great relief.

I remember one day when he brought me three pygmy shrews, one at a time, in less than thirty minutes. They were beautiful little creatures and I was so disappointed he had killed them.

Amazingly, one morning, he caught and killed a stoat. I can assure you not many cats are capable of doing this brave deed. Stoats are ferocious little animals and on a regular basis they kill full-grown rabbits which are four or five times bigger than themselves. I am sure that the one Mouse killed would have done its best to fend him off. But Mr Mouse was totally unmarked from his victorious battle with Mr Stoat.

A stoat, note it's fangs

Some interesting stoat and mustelid facts

Stoats are found throughout the northern hemisphere including, America, Europe, Great Britain, Canada, and Russia. Unfortunately, they were introduced to New Zealand in 1879 and have had a devasting effect on the bird population, especially the much-endangered kiwi. Their habitat is woodlands, grasslands, and wetlands.

The stoat is a small mammal that belongs to the mustelid family. The Mustelidae are a diverse family of carnivorous mammals that include weasels, (weasels are the smallest in the family) ferrets, martens, badgers, otters, and the fearless wolverine.

Wolverines are totally fearless and have been known to kill moose and caribou trapped in snow, which are far, far bigger than themselves. A wolverine weighs up to 66 pounds (almost 30 kg) and measures 17 inches (43.18 cm) at the shoulder. A moose is the largest and heaviest of all deer and a male weighs just over 1,543 pounds (700 kg) and stands 6 feet 8 inches (2.1 meters) at the shoulder.

Stoats are long and thin enabling them to enter holes frequented by their prey. They have short legs, small ears, and thick warm fur, and can grow to be as long as 12.8 inches or 32.15 centimeters. (More than a foot long.) They have a brown coat in summer and a white coat in winter. The tail has a black tip all the year round. The winter coat is called ermine. Ermine is the white fur with small black patches that historically has been sewn together for the collars on the robes worn by royalty and high-ranking peers.

Stoats are skilled super hunters and kill prey much larger than their-selves, such as rabbits. They also prey on other animals such as rats, mice, birds and lizards, and often store food for later. They are prolific climbers of trees where they gain access to birds' nests and are common raiders of nest boxes. They are known to mesmerize rabbits by enacting a complicated wriggling dance that is called the ‘weasel war dance’.

Stoats do not see colour as well as humans, but they can see better at night. They are not nocturnal and are most active during dawn and dusk. Like skunks, stoats can spray a bad-smelling fluid when they are scared.

In other words, you don’t mess about with stoats.

And you most certainly don’t mess about with wolverines!!!

A wolverine showing his worth

A bull moose

Now here is an amazing short story about

a determined female stoat. (Females are two inches smaller than the males.)

We had a quaint wooden bird table standing on the lawn at the back of the cottage. On it, Kathy had placed quite a large chunk of marzipan that was left over from a Christmas cake.

In absolute amazement, from our kitchen window, I observed a female stoat climbing four feet up the wooden stem of the bird table and then quite easily negotiating the overhang to reach and grab the marzipan. Clutching it in her tiny jaws, she struggled down backwards to eventually drop the short distance to the lawn. I could not believe what I was witnessing. The marzipan was half as big as her! Still with the marzipan clenched in her tiny jaws and holding it between her front legs, she reared up on her hind legs and with a wobbly walk she eventually disappeared with it through the beech hedge that surrounded the garden.

So, there you have it, a sweet-toothed stoat, probably taking the large chunk of marzipan to feed her off-spring. For sure, there is nothing as remarkable as nature.

Two normal visitors to the bird table. A nuthatch and a blue tit

After that interesting information about the Mustelidae family, let's get back to Mouse's story.

Mouse had an annoying habit of taking his flea-ridden trophies to the mesh-gated entrance of the cattery building. He was probably showing off his wares to the cats inside. With him roaming free, he probably regarded the cats residing inside as prison inmates!

One morning, I even found a full-grown hen pheasant lying dead by the cattery entrance gate. Perhaps he thought we were not feeding the guests enough, or maybe pheasant should have been put on their menu.

No wonder gamekeepers cull feral cats!

On one memorable occasion, I was in the cattery and witnessed Mouse arrive in front of the entrance dragging a full-grown very dead rabbit by its throat. He stood at the gate, peering in with the large rabbit still in his jaws, which I must add, was almost bigger than him.

I thought,

'Are you showing off that large trophy to make my guests jealous?'

After a few seconds, he released the rabbit and proceeded to roll on top of it.

I think he was saying to the prison inmates,

"Look what I've got. This one's mine. All mine."

I looked around the cattery to see quite a few pairs of jealous eyes looking out...

In envy?

'Perhaps I should be putting fresh rabbit on the menu?'

One of the cattery girls Jenny was nearby and was also watching Mouse's antics.

I said,

"Jen, can you please get me the flea spray?"

I knew that after rolling on the dead rabbit, Mouse would have been instantly infested with those nasty little parasites.

I hated Mouse taking his toll on all the lovely wildlife. People say it's only nature, but I strongly disagree. Domestic cats are not natural residents of the British Isles and they kill an unnecessary amount of wildlife, amounting to more than sixty million birds and mammals a year!

Can you believe that?

Sadly, I am afraid it is a fact!

Well, Mousey boy was in feline paradise on our grounds.

But soon his killing spree was to come to an abrupt end!!!

Here is some more interesting information from Geoff.

Many ex-gamekeepers, like myself, know an awful lot about wildlife and become strong conservationists, so you will see in my writing, where I am coming from. It is a fact the wildlife artist, Peter Scott, was originally a shooting man who turned into a strong conservationist and I am proud to be a member of that band. Oh, by the way, Peter is the son of the intrepid British explorer, Captain Scott of the Antarctic.

Ok, that's enough of that, let's get back to Mouse's story yet again.

I was doing some gardening one day and in one of our ornamental conifers, I discovered a well-hidden goldfinch's nest containing four nestlings. Goldfinches are one of Britain's most colourful little birds. Over the following week, I was so pleased to be able to observe the parents continuously racing back and forth with food for their rapidly growing offspring.

Right by our house as well!

At the end of the week, I was at the top of the garden. To my dismay, I heard the adult goldfinches making alarm calls. I walked over to the ornamental conifer to investigate what the chattering noise was all about. The beautiful pair of adult goldfinches were flitting about in total distress.

To my absolute horror and disappointment, I found all four of their nestlings lying dead at the base of the conifer. The nest that had been twelve feet above, had been dragged down and ransacked. The nestlings were lying nearby. I knew from my working experience as a gamekeeper that the little nestlings bore the teeth marks of a cat.

And there was only one cat living in the vicinity.

Guess who?

It could only have been the work of my mate Mouse, who at that moment, was far from being my mate. I was so angry with him. I informed Kathy of my gruesome find, and it upset her as well.

She said,

"Geoff. What can we do to stop him?"

I replied,

"The only way is to keep him inside."

She didn't like my answer and said,

"But that's cruel to lock him away, it would be like a prison!"

I responded,

"Not as cruel as the toll he's inflicting on the vulnerable wildlife around here!"

We didn't confine Mouse to his quarters right away, but we had many discussions about whether we should keep him inside or not.

The last straw happened very soon after his killing spree of the four nestling goldfinches.

One morning I was coming out of the cattery, only to see Mouse proudly walking toward me with his twitching tail raised vertically.

To my horror, in his mouth, he had a tiny fluffy mallard duckling, it didn't look to be more than two days old.

'OH, NO!'

'It's still alive!'

I tried to get close to Mouse, but he wouldn't come within touching distance of me. He most certainly intended to hang on to his prey. I clapped my hands loudly together and at the same time bellowed out angrily,

"DROP IT! DROP IT! YOU LITTLE SOD!"

Surprisingly enough he did, and the little duckling scurried into a nearby puddle of water. The poor tiny duckling in desperation to find sanctuary, tried to dive under the water. Unfortunately, the water was only two inches deep making submergence impossible.

THERE WAS NO ESCAPE!!!

The tiny duckling stood no chance. Before I could do anything, Mouse pounced like a ferocious tiger. He totally ignored the water and grabbed his tiny victim in his powerful jaws and ran off. In hot pursuit, I ran after him shouting angrily. (I won't mention what my words were!)

That was the last time I ever saw that tiny duckling.

AND THAT WAS THE LAST TIME MOUSE EVER MADE A KILL!!!

I was so angry with him!

That was the final straw!

So, from that day on, Mouse became a house cat.

We sprayed Mouse for fleas for the very last time, he would never have those horrible parasites on him ever again and as a bonus, no more tapeworms. Fleas bite cats and infect their bloodstream with tapeworm larvae. We could always tell when Mouse was carrying fleas because the fur on his ears was light-coloured, therefore it was easy to see black patches that represented clusters of fleas...

Yuk!

So, there was not going to be any more rabbits, pheasants, stoats, birds, mammals and certainly no more ducklings killed by Mr Mouse ever again.

Life was certainly going to be very different for

him in the future and more importantly the wildlife outside.

Mouse adapted to his new lifestyle very well. Occasionally, he meowed to go outside as he sat in our dining room looking through the patio window, but we just had to ignore him.

Then Kathy had an idea...

She bought him a harness and lead, so on sunny days we took him out for walks. He was quite amusing to watch as he strutted about raising his little pink nose in the air taking in all the sensuous aromas.

We noticed Mouse became a lot more lovable and, in the evenings, he fell asleep stretched out on one of our laps. He became totally dependent on us. He even watched TV, especially the animal and birdlife programmes presented by my hero, Sir David Attenborough. As soon as Mouse heard birds chirping, his little ears pricked up and his eyes opened wide almost shooting out of their sockets. With him being so transfixed, he dived toward the TV screen in a bid to catch the bird. His instincts never left him. It was so funny and entertaining seeing him run around the back of the TV, trying to find where the bird on the screen had disappeared to.

I used to play hide and seek with Mouse and chase him all around the inside of our cottage. He had favourite hiding places where he ambushed me, and as I got close to him, he jumped out at me. At times, the lovely lad reversed roles and chased me and then it was my turn to hide.

Oh, what fantastic fun we had!

On numerous occasions, as I relaxed in my favourite TV armchair watching the evening news, Mouse came tearing into the lounge at breakneck speed hitting the brakes and abruptly stopping right in front of me. For no more than a second, he stared right into my eyes. With that, he shot out again hoping I would give chase.

On other occasions, I could hear him running up the stairs, again at breakneck speed, jumping on and off the beds with great noisy thumps. You might have thought it was an elephant upstairs not a cat! Once he had completed his trampoline act on the beds, he thumped back down the stairs in only three bounds right back to where I was sitting and gave me yet another good hypnotic stare waiting for me to give chase. And then off he tore again on his circuit with me very often hot on his tail.

After the first few months, Mouse never appeared to miss going outside and I must say he was much healthier for it. I often think of the good times with him and that fateful day when I almost pulled the trigger.

As I stated before, one of the best decisions of my life.

So, Kathy and I had the wonderful privilege of meeting Mr Mouse and spending all those lovely years with him. His life with us was a very happy one, and most certainly it was for us. Mouse spent eleven years at Keepers Cottage, and when we retired and moved out to Spain, he came with us. He loved the sunshine and was allowed out onto the sunny terrace that he never strayed from.

Sadly, Mouse only spent his last two years of life enjoying the warmth and sunshine of Spain.

Early one morning, I had a massive shock!!!

With no warning of illness whatsoever, I found our poor Mousey dead in his bed. With tears in my eyes, I buried him in the shade, under the red spiky flowering bottle-brush tree in our Spanish garden.

CHAPTER 9

The Love of my Life and the Lustful Lab

Sally and Ricky

Have you ever gone to dinner parties where the hosts and guests more than often converse about their pets? Generally, they talk about cats and dogs. Well, that's one good reason why I wrote this book. Although I have never heard anyone talking about a pet goldfish!

Pet owners love to talk about their pets because to them they are unique. Some of the stories are interesting, but some can be unbelievably boring. Also, people get restless when they view too many of their friend's holiday snaps. Especially if they are not in them! Regarding myself, I call holiday snaps visitor repellents. I have found it is a good way of getting rid of dinner guests when it is late. They soon make a move when your holiday snaps come out!

Hopefully, this story is not boring, it is mainly about Sally, my Springer Spaniel. She was of the liver and white variety and no different to anyone else's dog. She was pretty similar in appearance to any Springer Spaniel, possessing a head, a body, four legs and a docked tail. But Sally was very special to me, very unique in many ways and became an important member of our family.

I was a gamekeeper when I acquired Sally and virtually bought her before even seeing her. I heard through the grapevine, via another gamekeeper about a litter of five pure-pedigree Springer Spaniels. One bitch and four dogs from champion parents. Immediately I made the phone call, and to cut a long conversation short.

I said,

"Can you please save the bitch for me?"

The last thing I wanted was another randy male, similar to the one in the next few paragraphs.

And here he is...

Randy Ricky!

My first gundog before Sally was a black Labrador. He was only eight weeks old when I acquired him and I named him

Ricky. I bought him from George Clarke a head gamekeeper who was originally from the county of Herefordshire.

Gamekeeping Facts

Years ago, a head gamekeeper was in charge of numerous under-keepers rearing thousands of pheasants and partridges, especially on royal estates. As well as producing a harvestable surplus of gamebirds, gamekeepers contribute to associated conservation activities for the benefit of other flora and forna. Besides rearing game birds, under-keepers were expected to undertake routine estate maintenance.

A gamekeeper wearing plus fours from years gone by

After that little glimpse about gamekeeping, here is an amusing short story about George.

George was a lovely man, a jovial country character with a strong Herefordshire accent from that lovely region. He was full of harmless mischief and with George, we never knew what sort of a prank he was going to pull next. I have to say, they certainly threw away the mould when they made him.

Whatever the weather, George always dressed very smart, wearing a tweed jacket, tie, waistcoat, plus fours and brown polished hob-nailed boots. George's best friend was another head gamekeeper, Harry Johnson, whom I met when I was fifteen years old. Harry turned out to be my hero and I worshipped the ground he walked on. I loved the tweedy attire of these old-school gamekeepers and I copied them by wearing the same type of rustic clothing.

I have a vivid memory of George when I played a game of cards with him and his young under-keeper, my friend Mac.

Can you believe this?

The game of cards took place in the middle of a

cornfield of standing barley!!!

I will never forget this vision…

A pack of cards floating and twirling away in the strong breeze as George hurled them high in the air.

Mac and I looked at each other in absolute amazement.

Then with a mischievous glint in his eye, Mac came out with this memorable comment,

"I don't think George is too happy with his hand!"

Readers might well ask,

"Why on earth were you playing cards in a cornfield?"

Well, George's army green Land Rover was parked nearby on the rearing field where he was supposedly working with the pheasant poults. George's wife Betty had a full view of the vehicle from their kitchen window. If she had found out that he was playing cards, instead of working, she would have killed him.

Well, boys will be boys.

Happy days!

Here is George with his eyes full of mischief in typical gamekeeping old school attire

Now back to Ricky.

If I had known how Ricky's character was going to turn out, I should have named him Randy! If a dog moved or even breathed, it didn't make any difference to Randy Ricky. Male or female, he tried to have his wicked way.

As a lustful lab, he was shoved off the backs of female dogs on too many occasions because it did not matter to him whether they were in season or not.

Ken, a gamekeeper friend of mine, was the owner of a black Labrador bitch called Meg. One day, Randy Ricky forced his wicked way on her before we could stop him. Ken was not a happy chappy! To calm him down, I offered to pay the bill for an injection to prevent Meg from getting pregnant. To my relief Ken accepted.

Two days after, to prevent her from being impregnated again, Meg who normally roamed free around the vicinity of Ken's cottage, was shut in her night-time run and sleeping quarters with a six-foot-high chain link fence.

But...

That fence did not stop the lust-crazed Labrador Ricky. He impregnated his victim, for the second time!!!

Amazingly, Randy Ricky full of lust managed

to scale the six-foot-high chain-link fence. This happened when we were inside Ken's cottage having a relaxing cup of tea. When we came out, we discovered them. The look on Ken's face was a picture! The couple were locked in love, standing back-to-back as mating dogs do.

That is probably where the phrase, 'Get knotted', comes from.

Ricky looked shattered, the black Labrador bitch looked embarrassed, and Ken was absolutely furious!

Ken snarled at me,

"That's twice in three days your randy dog has had my bitch. I've taken her to the vet once to prevent pregnancy. It won't be safe to have her injected again. He wants seeing too!"

I think he meant Ricky, not the vet!

What could I say, I felt so guilty.

Ricky had climbed over and done the dirty deed.

What could I do?

I apologised and grovelled profusely. If Ricky had

been capable of talking, it should have been him apologising, not me!

Ken, after a few minutes of ranting and raving, eventually calmed down.

The fact is, if a female dog has been accidentally mated, she can be administered an injection to stop her from conceiving. If she was mated again within days, the second injection could be fatal. So, the pregnancy just has to take its course. If the bitch was lucky, she would not be pregnant with the second unwanted mating.

But Ken's bitch was not so lucky!

As time, eventually proved...

Ricky, the Lustful Lab, sired five beautiful pedigree black Labrador puppies. Well, Ken was not too perturbed because Ricky had a good pedigree and so did Meg. Eventually, the five puppies were sold for a very good price, and Ken was smiling happily with the cash in his back pocket. He wasn't exactly forthcoming in offering me the pick of the litter, which is the normal procedure for the owner of the male dog. Not that I wanted one, but the cash would have been greatly appreciated. So, Ricky the proud father and I just kept stumm.

Because of Ricky's amorous adventures, I was very fortunate not to lose Ken as a friend, especially as we had known each other for many years. At least, that was a happy ending to one of 'Randy Ricky's' dirty deeds.

Also, Ricky embarrassed me on numerous occasions involving friends and even strangers by cocking his leg up against them and peeing on their legs. It got even worse when he wrapped his front legs around them and started to gyrate. Gender didn't seem to matter to him, but it was terribly embarrassing for me, especially when his target happened to be a lady whom I didn't even know!

Shortly after the saga with Ken's bitch, I spoke to the vet about Ricky's over-sexual nature and he suggested castration. I didn't like the sound of that. And I am sure neither did Ricky!

The other option was a new procedure. It was to insert two caponising tablets into the back of Ricky's neck. And that is what I decided on.

The tablets caused Ricky to produce female hormones for eighteen months. The poor lad just couldn't understand why he was attracting so much sexual attention from the male gender of his species. Mind you he had grown quite large teats!

All the gamekeepers certainly laughed at that one. Especially Ken!

But the good news was, it worked.

Well, good old Ricky managed to attain the grand old age of twelve, which wasn't bad for a working Labrador. As you can imagine, having been a gundog and a sex maniac as well, he had led quite an active life. In the winter of his life Randy Ricky had suffered a few minor heart attacks and according to my vet, that is quite normal for dogs. Unlike humans, a lot of dogs bounce back almost as if nothing has happened. Some dogs can carry on for years, it is quite amazing the stamina some of them have. But sadly, my poor old Ricky didn't last too long after his first major coronary. Two years before his health issues, Ricky had the good fortune to meet Sally.

So, after that amusing black Labrador story, let us move on to the love of my life, Sally.

Sally

I will always remember that it was a very cold February day with light snow flurries when I had arranged to pick up little Sally from the breeder. Driving down the narrow country lanes was quite challenging with the roads being so slippery and covered in frozen tyre-crunching snow. But I most certainly was not going to let that stop me. I just couldn't wait to see Sally.

Eventually, I arrived at my destination, knocked on the door and was shown in by Patricia the breeder. Patricia who liked to be called Trish showed me the litter of puppies. Generally, all puppies are lovely, but the one that really stood out in this litter was Sally. Instantly, I fell in love with her. She was only nine weeks old, perfectly marked in liver and white with a thin white blaze running down the centre of her face. She could only be described as cute.

Not that looks had mattered to 'Randy Ricky'!

I knew I would have to guard my little Sally very carefully against the amorous advances from the lustful devil. The last thing I wanted was a litter of mongrel crosses. As it turned out, Sally could handle herself and warned Ricky in no uncertain terms that she was not available under any circumstances. Every time he tried to get his wicked way, there was a snap and a snarl from Sally, with a flash and click of her white teeth and a loud cowardly yelp from the optimistic offender. Throughout her life that was the only aggression she ever showed.

Only three days before 'Randy Ricky' died he still had designs on impregnating my Sally, who at that time was only eighteen months old. Now that's what you call stamina!

Sally's temperament was outstanding. She was incredibly intelligent, which was fortunate for me because it enabled me to train her very easily as a gundog. She soon obeyed the commands from my plastic whistle, even at long distances. One blast for sit, and three blasts for come. Sally, like all the Springer breed, was fearless of the thorniest thickets and she went through them as if she had the skin of a rhinoceros.

Sally's memory was amazing too. She even knew when to protect pheasants, rather than hunt them.

When the pheasant chicks were tiny, they are just like cute two-legged bumblebees. Every evening the chicks needed to be shooed into the eight heated plywood brooder sheds that adjoined the thirty-by-thirty-foot wire netting pens.

Tiny pheasant chicks are very well camouflaged therefore, they could quite easily have been missed as they instinctively squatted down in the pen in the long grass. If we had missed any and they were left out overnight, they would surely have died from the cold. In the brooder shed, there was a gas heater suspended eighteen inches from the floor, it gave off heat (90 degrees Fahrenheit/32 degrees Celsius) just like a brooding hen pheasant in the wild.

In spring on the rearing field, Sally really came into her own.

From year to year, as soon as Sally arrived outside the gates of the freshly erected sheds and pens, she sprang up and down almost three feet off the ground in her excitement and anticipation to be let in.

Hence the name, Springer Spaniel.

The rearing field

Sally's job was to seek out the chicks that I had overlooked. She pointed them out with her nose, whilst raising her front paw. This is known as the 'pointing stance'. It is a term used in the gundog world. Very gently she picked them up in her mouth and retrieved them totally unharmed, enabling me to put them in the warm shed for the night. Pheasants needed to be shut away every night, right up to the age of four weeks and by this time they were called poults. Sally and I enjoyed working close to nature and did this particular job for nine consecutive summers.

Above, a cute day-old pheasant chick followed by a beautiful adult male

One August weekend, we were visited by friends, a couple from Cheshire, Pete and Sue, they worked in the same complex as Kathy, belonging to Barclays Bank known as, Radbroke Hall. They were into golf in a big way and they tried to teach us how to hit golf balls. At that tie Kathy and I had no idea about golf and didn't know one end of the golf club from the other. Now that I do play golf, my friend's joke and say, I still don't! Well, I think they were only joking!

To demonstrate how to hit a golf ball, Pete hit twelve balls down the twenty-acre grass field situated behind our cottage. I was quite impressed with the distance that Pete hit the balls, although I had never seen anyone hit a golf ball before. As usual, Sally was close by, and I must say was looking rather bored with the proceedings.

I am sure she must have been thinking,

'I don't like this new kind of gun.'

After a while, she trotted off to her favourite place on the mat outside our back door, where I am sure she was dreaming of much better things, such as pheasants and partridges.

Not boring golf balls!

After Pete hit the balls, the four of us trailed down the field to look for them and after searching for at least half an hour, we could only find one.

It sure looked like an expensive sport to me! Pete seemed to have hit the balls in more or less the same area, but we didn't seem to stand ‘A cat in hell’s chance' of finding any of them. The grass was only three inches deep, but the base was thick with clover.

I came up with an idea, and said,

"Pete, I think I know how we can find these balls."

With that, I blew three high-pitched peeps on my plastic dog whistle which was always hanging around my neck. On hearing the sound, just like the Lone Ranger's horse Silver, Sally sped flat out toward me. Within seconds she pulled up at my feet in docked tail-wagging excitement.

In anticipation, she looked up at me with her eager brown eyes, as if to say,

"What can I do for you now Master?"

I asked Pete to hand me the only ball that we had managed to find. I held it under Sally’s nose for her to sniff the new scent. She wagged her docked tail even more furiously. I extended my right arm and pointed my finger in the direction of the missing golf balls.

I said,

"Get on Sal. Good dog. Fetch."

With her nose to the ground, Sally rocketed off with her rump high in the air excitedly wagging it from side to side. Within thirty seconds she was retrieving her very first golf ball. She arrived at my feet and placed it in my hand, just as if it was an egg or a tiny pheasant chick. Pete stared in absolute amazement.

He said,

"I don't believe what I'm seeing!"

I sent Sally out to retrieve more golf balls, one after the other and she was really showing off her skills. Pete and Sue had never seen a gundog work before and they were more than impressed with Sally's demonstration.

Pete said,

"Wait until I tell my friends at the golf club about Sally retrieving these golf balls. They will want to offer her a job. We lose balls every day!"

Sally retrieved the remaining balls in less than ten minutes and we knew we were not going to lose any more, especially with her as backup. Many more were hit down the field and Sally was in her element.

By then, Sally was really interested in this new type of gun. The golf club!

When it was mine and Kathy's turn, the golf balls were hit all over the place, not unlike the way I play today! Military golf they call it, left, right, left, right, left, right. Perhaps I am being hard on myself, but I do manage to hit them straight occasionally.

Sally turned out to be a legend in her own time and my shooting associates kept pestering me with similar requests,

"If ever you breed from Sally, please let me know. I would love to buy one of her pups."

So, I decided that when Sally was six years old, we would breed some little Sallys.

Eventually, Sally was mated with a Springer Spaniel named Rufus. He had an excellent pedigree, so I planned to keep two of the puppies.

But only if they were bitches. No more 'Randy Ricky's' for me, thank you very much. For sure, any puppies that were left would have been sold many times over.

Six weeks into the gestation period, Sally looked well pregnant and we couldn't wait to meet her puppies.

But she fooled us all…

It was a phantom pregnancy!

'ARGHHH!'

Frustratingly, we had to wait another six months until she came in season again before she was ready for another amorous meeting with Rufus.

After the second renaissance, I was determined that she was not going to fool us again, so I had her examined by our veterinary surgeon. It was great news she was confirmed pregnant.

THE PUPPIES ARRIVE!

Early one morning, Kathy checked on Sally in her sleeping quarters and noticed that she was acting rather strangely. By the time Kathy had rushed and fetched me from our cottage, Sally had given birth to her first pup. We watched the rest being born and found it amazing just how she knew exactly what to do. She bit off each umbilical cord and then licked the puppy clean. In between each birth, she even found time to look up at us, as she proudly wagged her stumpy tail.

Sally produced five beautiful liver and white puppies, four females and one male.

We kept two of the bitches and named them, Jess and Jemma. The male puppy was given free to the owner of Rufus and we sold the two remaining bitches to two friends whose names were at the top of the long list.

Sally was nine years old when I started building the cattery and kennels, and she became semi-retired from the shooting world. Although we still went shooting once a week during the gamebird season, she was getting past her prime. She started to put on weight and had got a little bit naughty where food was concerned. Her main hobby became eating. She went to great lengths to steal food and I kept a close eye on her because being overweight was not good for an ageing Springer Spaniel or any other breed.

Two bricklayers, Eric and John were

constructing the buildings for our new cattery and kennels. Because of Sally's greedy habits, I warned them to keep their sandwiches safely locked away in their van. During their lunch breaks, crafty Sally knew exactly what time the breaks were and had a routine of turning up and begging by using her gorgeous hypnotic brown eyes. Unfortunately, Eric and John could not resist her bewitching pleas. So, Sally always walked away triumphantly with her rump wagging and a sandwich in her mouth. This was seriously against my wishes, but I am sure they must have thought that the way she begged, I was starving her to death.

One morning, Eric and John left their sandwiches in the van, but unfortunately, they had carelessly left a side window open. All Sally had to do was follow her keen nose that picked up the tempting aromas. When no one was around she dived straight through the open window. It was certainly no problem at all for a gundog such as Sally with her experience of clearing high fences. Once inside the van, she located the delicious sandwiches and wolfed the lot down.

The fat little pig certainly gorged herself that day!

To put it mildly, Eric and John were not exactly

over the moon.

When I found out what the cute little thief had done, I am afraid I did not have too much sympathy with Eric and John.

I said,

"Well, you can't say I didn't warn you. She's not as innocent as you think!"

Unfortunately, they had learnt the hard way.

Well, I did the honourable thing and went down to the cottage and made them some sandwiches. I must add, that was a traumatic event for me because Kathy, who was out at the time, always spoiled me by making my sandwiches.

So that was a very rare event indeed!

Eventually, when the cattery and kennels opened, Sally was always by my side, keenly greeting our new customers. It was guaranteed that they booked their pets in as she rolled over on her back and enjoyed being fussed, patted and stroked.

I am sure Sally was the best public relations officer ever!

CHAPTER 10

When Arthur met Sally

A story which features, of all things, a bean bag!

One morning, a customer arrived delivering Arthur, a light brown pampered Great Dane. Arthur was as big a Great Dane as you were ever likely to see, in fact, he was absolutely enormous. He was almost as big as a donkey. We christened him King Arthur because he was so big and aristocratic and always arrived in a brand-new Range Rover, as royalty do.

We had another owner who boarded two of the giant dogs with us. Because of their black and white patchwork colouring, they were a very special type of Great Dane, known as 'Harlequins'. I have to admit, those two dogs were gorgeous and because of their colour and size, it looked like we had a pair of Friesian cows on leads!

Great Dane Facts

The Great Dane is a very large dog originating from Germany. The breed descends from hunting dogs dating from the Middle Ages. They were used for hunting deer and wild boar. Also, they were used for guarding nobility. It is one of the two largest breeds in the world, the other one is the Irish Wolfhound. Male Great Danes weigh up to 175lb. I weigh 143lb, this gives you an idea of just how big and heavy they are.

A Great Dane the same colour as Arthur

A Harlequin Great Dane

Have you ever tried walking one Great Dane on a lead, let alone two? I can assure you it was an absolute nightmare.

Having experienced hanging onto Arthur at my peril after he had spotted a rabbit in the woodland, I thought I was being dragged by a four-wheel-drive tractor, not a dog! Unfortunately for me, I always walked him with me being the strongest person on the premises and probably the foolhardiest.

Here comes the bean bag...

Due to Arthur's size and weight, his owner always brought him a large bean bag to sleep on.

The bean bag was necessary to stop Arthur from getting bedsores because he spent a lot of time lying down as all heavy Great Danes do. The bean bag had been dumped unceremoniously by his owner on the concrete path outside the office door. This was right next to where Sally was dozing in her usual spot minding her own business.

Arthur had met Sally many times before, but on this particular day, he seemed to be in a bad mood. Perhaps it was because Sally was curled up too close to his bean bag, I had no idea what the cause was. As Arthur jumped out of the vehicle, fortunately still on his lead with me grimly hanging on to the other end, he made an aggressive lunge toward my Sally.

I could barely hang on to the massive brute, he was far bigger and heavier than me. He dragged me along toward Sally as if I was not there. Submissively whimpering, Sally rolled over onto her back showing absolutely no aggression at all. The big bully tried to rough her up but I just managed to drag him off her as she screamed blue murder. Thankfully her screaming put him off his attack.

Arthur's owner shouted at him for being a bad boy. Luckily, there was no damage done, except maybe to Sally's pride. It was lucky for Arthur that he hadn't hurt my precious Sally, because if he had done, I would have felt like shooting the big bullying brute. Well, I didn't shoot him, I just dragged him around the corner of the kennel buildings to take him into the wood for his walk. At least the one good thing was, I had a safe walk with no unplanned incidents.

Thank goodness the big boy didn't see any rabbits!

That would have been the last straw.

I installed King Arthur into his kennel and went into the office to have a word with Kathy, who had witnessed the fracas when she was doing some paperwork.

I asked,

"Where's Sally?"

"Oh, don't worry she's okay, she's just gone down to the cottage. But have I got some amusing news for you!"

"What do you mean?"

"Well, Arthur's owner was very apologetic for Arthur's boisterous behaviour."

"BOISTEROUS! BOISTEROUS! I have seen tanks in war films put to shame in comparison to that brute!"

"Calm down Geoff. Listen to what I have to tell you. You are going to laugh at this."

"Okay, okay, carry on."

"Well, I looked through the window and Sally was licking her coat as if she was wounded. Suddenly, she got up and shook herself, had a sniff at Arthur's bean bag. And what do you think she did next?"

"Well, come on tell me."

"She squatted with one of her back legs raised high in the air and did a small pee right in the centre of Arthur's bean bag. She looked just like a male dog marking his territory. Then she calmly sauntered off down to the cottage with her nose held high in the air."

On hearing this I was astonished, Sally had never, ever cocked her leg in the air when she had a pee. I am sure she had done the amusing deed as if to say to Arthur,

"That'll teach you for attacking me, you big bully!"

I examined the bean bag where Sally had made her mark and there was no more than a teaspoonful.

'Good girl Sal, that'll teach that great lummox a lesson.'

So why did Sally do it?

To me, it was the only way she could pay Arthur back, I am sure she must have thought every time the big brute lay on his bed, he would smell her urine. Sally, the little dog that never did him, or any other dog any harm would remind Arthur of his bad behaviour toward, 'Sally Queen of the kennels'.

So, little Queen Sally ended up being the ruler over the giant King Arthur.

I don't know if Arthur had thought that it was me who had put Sally up to peeing on his bean bag, but payback time very nearly came for me...

FRIGHTENINGLY!

After three weeks of walking Arthur twice a day, the big boy had grown on me, even though he had upset my Sally. We appeared to be very good mates and when it came to the day for Arthur to leave, I must admit, I was quite sad as I led him out of the kennel block toward the waiting Range Rover.

The tail door was open and the giant dog jumped in. I let go of his lead and reached out to stroke his head which I had done many times before.

SUDDENLY!

With absolutely no warning at all.

Arthur lunged at me.

WITH TEETH FLASHING.

He very nearly ripped my hand off!

If it hadn't been for my quick reflexes, I would have been a hospital case. My previous best mate, now a big ungrateful brute, had missed me by a hair's breadth.

Arthur's unconcerned owner, who had obviously seen the same performance before said,

"Oh, he gets a bit possessive now and again, especially when he is in his own vehicle."

'A bit possessive! A bit possessive! The big brute nearly took my hand off up to my armpit!'

Well, they do say 'You live and learn' something every day. I can assure you it was the very last time I tried to stroke any dog in its owner's car.

Arthur met Sally many more times after the bean bag event and King Arthur always showed Sally the utmost respect, which the great lady deserved.

But of course, with me being biased…

Sally was the Queen of all dogs!

CHAPTER 11

A Traumatic Event and a Fishy Tail

All the fun of expanding a pet hotel business with a lucky escape and a high jumper.

The first story revolves around a mate of mine, Pete.

Pete was a bricklayer and with his skills in the building trade, he could just about turn his hand to anything and he was a great help to me on many occasions.

BUT, THERE IS ONE DANGEROUS OCCASION, BOTH OF US WILL NEVER EVER FORGET...

Pete was in his mid-fifties, he had a weathered brown face, blue eyes and black-grey-flecked combed-back hair. He stood around five-eight, carrying a stout, stocky build and was as strong as an ox.

With us being inundated with bookings, I decided to expand the business and build another large kennel block. Pete and I had just finished laying several lorry loads of ready-mix concrete in a fifty-five-yard long strip, five yards wide and six inches deep.

Having straightened our aching backs, we were chatting and admiring our handiwork, meaning the shiny strip of wet concrete gleaming in the sunshine. The backbreaking work of laying concrete when it has just been finished always gave me complete job satisfaction and this day was no exception. The unblemished concrete strip looked as smooth as silk.

UNFORTUNATELY, THIS WAS NOT GOING TO LAST FOR LONG!

I clambered into bed at 9 pm that night, absolutely shattered and as soon as my head touched the pillow I went out like a light. I slept like a log happily dreaming about long silky strips of unblemished concrete. At 6.30 am I woke up feeling quite drowsy and dragged my muscle-aching limbs out of bed. The very first thing I did every morning was to look out of our back bedroom window and appreciate the beautiful panoramic view of green farmland stretching into the far-off distance.

I shouted,

"OH NO!"

Unfortunately, my instinctive explosive shout woke Kathy.

Quite startled, she asked,

“Whatever’s wrong”?

“I’ll tell you what’s wrong. It’s been raining, that’s what! And it looks like it’s been heavy”!

“So what’s the problem”?

“The problem is, it could have damaged the concrete Pete and I broke our backs over yesterday!”

My observation put me in a very frustrated mood. I showered quickly and with no breakfast inside me, I shot down to the kennels, hopefully to find no damage to the concrete.

When I saw what lay in front of my eyes, I could have cried.

I about-turned and sprinted to my office. I snatched the phone out of its cradle and punched in Pete’s number.

After thirty long seconds, he answered sleepily,

“Hello?”

“PETE, PETE ITS GEOFF!”

"What's up, mate?"

“We’ve got a big, big problem with the concrete.”

“What sort of a problem?”

“Last night we had heavy rain.”

“OH JESUS!!! I’m on my way.”

Pete lived just three miles down the road in Newport, and within ten minutes he pulled into our car park in his navy blue van. I was standing in front of the office.

He jumped out and calmly said,

"Ok, let's check the damage."

Walking with fast strides we arrived at the long strip of concrete.

The once silky smooth concrete looked as if some swine had flown over slowly in a hot air balloon and riddled it with millions and millions of bullets.

IT WAS POCKMARKED ALL OVER!

Pete knelt down and put the flat of his hand on the damaged surface.

Quite cool and calmly he said,

“It hasn’t gone off yet, if we act quickly, we might just be able to save the surface.”

“Pete you’re a magician! What’s the plan?”

Pete explained that concrete takes twenty-eight days to reach its full effective strength and in the building trade, they use the term, ‘Gone Off’. Our concrete strip was less than twenty-four hours old, which was still soft in comparison and hard enough to walk on. So, it had not ‘Gone Off’ completely.

Pete’s plan was to hire a small machine called a floor grinder. With a bit of luck, it might be able to smooth out the surface of the concrete strip before it went too hard. Pete gave me the name of the only tool hire company he knew that supplied them. I ran into my office and flicked quickly through the Yellow Pages. Thankfully I found them.

But, I was not so thankful with my telephone conversation...

The lady on the other end of the line informed me,

"Sorry sir, they are all hired out."

Shocked I replied,

"Oh no! I've got concrete going off. I'm desperate, I need one today. What am I going to do?"

Her response was favourable,

"Well, I might just be able to help you. We do have an old out-of-date machine, which we don't hire out these days because it is so old. I can let you have that one for free, providing you use it at your own risk."

I couldn't believe my luck, but little did I know that my good luck was going to turn into bad luck.

VERY BAD LUCK!!!

I drove the twelve-mile round trip like 'A bat out of hell' and presented Pete with the machine that was hopefully going to perform a miracle.

He took one look at it and said,

"Jesus Christ, I haven't seen one of these for years. I thought they went out with the Ark. No wonder you got it for free!"

The ancient grey-coloured machine was powered by petrol and to start it we had to pull a cord violently with a wooden handle. The machine looked like a large fan enclosed in a guard. The guard consisted of five rows of rounded safety bars on the top, forming a circle. The diameter of the machine was three feet across.

The guard was designed to stop the operator's foot from going through. There was no doubt in my mind that if someone's foot slipped in between the protective bars, it would be sliced to bits by three rapidly spinning four-inch-wide blades. Attached to the sides of the machine, angling upwards was a four-foot-long handle. The rubber-clad top of the handle was about thirty inches across. To operate the machine you gripped the wide handle, so you would be able to push or pull the machine in whatever direction you chose. It was a bit like using a lawnmower, but a lot heavier, therefore less manoeuvrable.

It took both of us to lift and carry the heavy machine to the waiting concrete. Amazingly, with Pete's very first pull on the starting cord, the old machine fired up. As the old machines scraping blades whirred into life, the noise was deafening.

I could see Pete was having a devil of a job to hold and control the vibrating grinder. I watched him for about five minutes and he seemed to be getting the hang of it. After about half an hour, I could see Pete was tiring. With caution, I gave him a very wide birth and walked around him to attract his attention. Waving my hands in a criss-cross fashion, I signalled him to turn the noisy machine off, which he did by flicking a switch that cut off the fuel supply.

I volunteered to have a go and Pete with heavy sweat running off his forehead gladly accepted my offer.

He said,

"This thing is a beast, but it seems to be doing a good job."

I took over the reins and like Pete, initially I struggled and wasn't sure who was in control...

THE BEAST, OR ME!

Throughout the morning Pete and I took turns to give each other a well-deserved break.

And thank goodness lunchtime was approaching.

During lunchtimes, Pete liked to sit in his van on the car park watching our customers coming and going. They were delivering and collecting their cats or dogs as he was eating his sandwiches. Pete's sandwiches on this particular day were provided by Kathy, not me, who by now worked full-time in our business.

I walked down to the cottage for my lunch and after a bit of a doze, I was ready for more action.

LITTLE DID I KNOW THAT I WAS HEADING FOR THE HOSPITAL ON THAT SUNNY AFTERNOON!

With renewed energy, I walked back up to the kennels and was raring to go. I could hear Pete already operating the grinder. When I walked up to the troublesome strip of concrete, he had his back to me.

I wanted to attract his attention and like a fool

standing right behind him, I bellowed,

"PETE!"

Immediately, Pete spun around.

And with him...

To my horror...

SO DID THE SCREAMING GRINDER!

Pete lost control...

THE OLD GRINDER SWERVED, SLID AND CAREERED TOWARD ME...

STRAIGHT AT ME...

'OH NO!'

Trying to get out of its way...

I jumped in the air...

I landed with my right foot safely on the concrete.

But...

My poor left foot was not so lucky…

It landed on top of the guard…

And then…

Slid straight through…

Right through…

Straight into the path of the flashing spinning blades…

'Jesus Christ!'

I screamed in agony.

ARGHHHHH!!!

And terror.

ARGHHHHH!!!

The blades had got my left leg, jammed just above my ankle.

Thinking I was losing my foot, Pete's face had gone as white as a sheet.

Immediately, Pete went down on his knees and tried to release my foot.

I screamed at him...

"NEVER MIND MY FOOT, TURN THE THING OFF!"

Eventually, he did!

My lower leg just above my ankle was completely jammed. It felt like it was in the grip of a great white shark.

And to my horror, my foot was in an abnormally twisted position.

It took the white-faced Pete, almost three long minutes to release my damaged leg.

I was in severe pain.

Amazingly, there was no blood.

Clear fluid was seeping out of two-deep indentations on either side of my leg, just above the ankle. The two-round indentions were almost an inch in diameter and I wasn't sure if I had broken any bones or not. To my utmost relief, I hadn't lost my foot and I could waggle it a little bit.

It hurt like crazy.

With Pete's support, I managed to limp back to the cottage only to be greeted by a horrified Kathy.

With a very concerned look on her shocked face, she sternly said,

"What on earth have you done now?"

Quickly I explained all the horrifying details of the accident.

I said,

"I can still walk. I'll be all right. Don't worry, I'm ok."

"Oh no, you're not!"

As I gasped and winced in pain. Gently, she examined my weeping leg.

Sternly she said,

"I'm taking you to the hospital, RIGHT NOW."

And you don't mess with Kathy!

Our nearest hospital was at Telford, twelve miles away. Kathy drove my black Toyota Land Cruiser at a fair old lick as I lay reclined in the passenger seat elevating my leg. As she drove, I watched the tops of green-leafed trees flying by, silhouetted against the cloudless blue sky.

In a tyre screeching stop we arrived at the emergency entrance of the hospital.

Immediately, I was helped into a wheelchair by a hospital porter. Feeling like an invalid I was pushed inside as Kathy parked the Cruiser.

Sitting in the wheelchair with my foot elevated on a free-standing chair, miraculously, I only had to wait thirty minutes. The porter pushed me into an examination room and helped me on to a couch. Within a minute a young Indian doctor breezed in.

With a pleasant smile on his face, he said,

So what have you been up to?

I joked,

"I have been experimenting with a new way of amputating my leg."

He laughed and said,

"Ok, let's have a look."

He gently gave my leg and ankle a thorough examination.

He said,

"Luckily, I don't think you have broken anything, but we'll have it X-rayed just in case."

Sitting in my wheelchair, I went for an X-ray.

After being X-rayed, I waited only a short time, before the young doctor returned with a big smile on his face and said,

"You have been a very, very lucky man. Your leg is not broken, but you do need to elevate it and rest for a few days, to let the internal bruising come out. If you had been a child with less muscle and a thinner boned leg, you most certainly would have lost the lower part of your leg and foot."

I think I already knew that!

After thanking the doctor profusely, Kathy drove me home whilst giving me a lecture on how I needed to take things easier in the future. As we turned into our drive, I persuaded her to drive me on to the car park which she reluctantly did. We parked up and Erica, our new manager came running out of the office to see if I was ok.

Kathy rolled her eyes, as I said to Erica,

"I'm feeling great. No problem! What happened with Pete? Did he finish the job?"

Erica replied,

"Yes he has. He finished the job about thirty minutes ago. He said he would be over the moon if he never clapped eyes on that horrible machine again and he has gone home because he didn't feel at all well. I have to say, he did look as white as a ghost."

I laughed and said,

"My accident has affected him more than me."

With that remark, Kathy rolled her eyes again and said,

"Come on hero. Let's get you back to the cottage."

Kathy wanted me to go straight back to the cottage to rest and put my leg up, but I had to see what the concrete looked like. Other than it being covered with concrete dust it did look quite smooth.

Eventually, Kathy drove me right up to our garden gate and helped me hobble up the path to the front door. I hopped into the cottage and hiding my pain, I crawled up the stairs to have a long soak in the bath. Then I did as everyone had commanded. I sprawled myself out and elevated my foot on the lounge settee in front of the TV.

I phoned Pete, to give him the good news about how my hospital visit had gone. I also explained it was not his fault, it was mine because I had startled him from behind and I should have known better.

The next day Pete turned up, with his face reverted back to its normal colour. He borrowed one of the power hoses from the kennels to use on the new concrete strip and hosed off all the dust created by the rogue grinder. I persuaded a reluctant Kathy to run me down to the kennels to see the finished work.

She said,

"I suppose I'll have to because I know you will never settle until you see that concrete."

As soon as I arrived at the kennels, Pete shook my hand vigorously and greeted me as if I had just come back from the dead.

He said,

"Thank goodness you are ok. I thought I had cut your foot off. After you went to the hospital, I felt really ill. It must have been the shock, even though you rang, I didn't get a wink of sleep last night."

I looked at the concrete strip and said,

"Well, thanks for finishing it off mate. What do you think?"

He enthusiastically replied,

"Smooth as a baby's bum. That's what I think. A job in the town mate!"

So with that last Shropshire saying, from my good mate Pete, concludes the story on how I almost lost my foot.

And to this very day, I still have the scars to prove it.

The Pond

Can a koi carp pond give you stress?

Now that is an interesting question.

Well, I had always fancied having a fish pond.

On a weekly basis, I transported the rubbish down to the local refuse centre. On this particular day, I noticed a small green fibreglass moulded base. It was kidney-shaped and I realised it was designed for a garden pond. So I rescued it and took it home.

Hence, the idea of building a garden pond was born.

And so was the idea of a second pond.

A bigger one.

A MUCH, MUCH, BIGGER ONE!

The big one comes along, just a little later.

Using the rescued base, I attempted to build a tiny pond.

My idea was to build a small waterfall using sandstone rock. It would be situated in a quiet corner of our front garden, up against our beautiful beech hedge. Well, I did succeed, but it took me all day to painstakingly build it.

ACTUALLY, IT TOOK TEN HOURS!

I must say, it did look a very professional job.

But...

It wasn't too long before I was extremely disappointed.

The waterfall leaked!

I was very, very frustrated with my apparent good work and my wasted precious time. I decided to ask my good friend Pete to come and have a look at my proud handiwork and give me some advice.

He came out with three words,

"Knock it down!"

And that is exactly what he did.

Within minutes!!!

'ARGHHH'

Pete was an expert at laying bricks, blocks, stone, you name it, and he rebuilt the waterfall in an amazing two hours.

Yes, only two hours and it had been ten precious wasted hours for me!

And, it never leaked in all the time we lived at Keepers Cottage. In other words, if you want a job done quickly and correctly, my advice is, to save valuable time, get a professional tradesman in.

Now here comes the second pond...

THE BIG ONE!

The big one, besides being filled with water was going to be filled with Koi carp. It was going to be bigger than many private swimming pools that lucky expats had in Spain. My second kidney-shaped pond was going to be at least sixty feet by thirty feet. It wasn't going to take me long to excavate the large hole because I was going to hire a Hymac excavator.

A Hymac is a very large, very powerful excavating machine that moves on tank tracks. At the front of the machine, there is a long extending arm that has a large bucket on the end. I have to say they are expensive to hire but boy do they move earth quickly.

The massive hole that was to be dug out would be situated in front of our cottage, on the large lawned area to the left of the cattery building. Fifteen cat runs extended from the side of the building. My idea was to give the cats a tantalising view of Koi carp gliding just under the surface of the water. Also, potential customers walking between the Koi pond and the cattery building would be impressed.

The massive bright yellow Hymac arrived outside the cattery on a truck called a low-loader and was expertly disembarked in rapid time. I gave the machine operator my simple instructions and he began the work straight away.

The hole was dug in two levels. This was to establish a depth of three feet of water at one level and six feet for the other. The deeper part would keep a little warmer in the winter, therefore protecting the fish from the freezing cold.

The unwanted soil from the excavated hole was quickly loaded by the machine's large bucket into a waiting lorry and carted away to a nearby farmer. With all the modern equipment involved, I knew this would take no time at all.

It was a very hot summer's day when we were digging out the hole for the pond. It was so dry, even when the excavator had gone down six feet, the soil was fine dust just like talcum powder. We never found one lowly earthworm until we reached the very bottom of the hole where there was a little moisture. Until that day, I never knew earthworms could burrow down so deep, but I suppose that beautiful rare summer the poor little chaps had no choice.

I certainly got my money's worth because it only took the powerful machine half a day to dig out the massive hole.

The next job was to line the pond with heavy-duty polythene, which I did. It was followed by a six-inch covering of ready-mix concrete. I will give you one guess who was going to spread the concrete.

Having personally laid over fifty lorry loads of the stuff over the years, I had counted them in bed, when most people count sheep! I didn't think I would have much of a problem.

BUT, HOW WRONG CAN ONE BE?

The day the concrete lorry arrived was yet another very hot day. In fact, it was incredibly hot. The ready-mix lorry turned up and the concrete was poured into the large hole.

All I had to do was level it to the shape of the hole.

Easy!

Or was it?

Unfortunately, I had a problem, the ready mix driver had not added enough water and it was far too dry, making it very hard to manoeuvre around with my shovel and rake. After three hours of grafting and grinding in the baking heat, I was sweating like a racehorse competing in the Grand National.

The concrete was going off, as I explained earlier, setting and going hard.

In fact, very hard.

Far too fast for my liking.

Especially, with my rapidly waning energy level.

I was getting in a right pickle and my Wellington boots were getting harder to pull out of the sucking concrete.

I needed help.

I was desperate.

I needed rescuing.

I was getting pretty well exhausted, to say the least, and had virtually run out of energy on that very hot day. Valiantly, Kathy tried to help me, but we were getting nowhere fast, or should I say, deeply in the mire. Kathy, against my stubborn protests, decided she was going to get help. She phoned my ex-gamekeeper mate, Fred, who lived just two miles down the road.

And thank goodness she did!

The cavalry duly arrived in the form of Fred, who was now a Park Ranger on the neighbouring country estate. Besides myself, another gamekeeper turned conservationist. I thought he would be busy enough doing his own job, but as usual, he didn't mind helping me as he had done many times in the past. In fact, we frequently helped each other out.

Here comes a bit of excitement...

On one occasion, I made the headlines in the local newspaper. On a cold winter night, I apprehended a legendary pheasant poacher. The guy who shall remain nameless was shooting roosting pheasants on Fred's estate.

But that is another story!

Anyway, back to my current concrete problem.

On this particular day, Fred most certainly saved my bacon. Subsequently, with his arrival, Kathy and I found renewed energy and the three of us finished the job in less than an hour. The saying, 'Many hands make light work', was most certainly true that day.

If Fred hadn't turned up, Kathy and I would have remained in that large hole to this very day, set in concrete.

Building the sides of the pond was the next job. I wanted them vertical in rendered brick because I knew that herons would turn up as soon as there were fish in the water. The vertical walls were necessary because herons prefer wading into shallow water with a gradual slope, so with my pond that would be impossible. Herons can certainly be a nightmare where ornamental ponds are concerned, unfortunately, they are experts at guzzling down tons of valuable Koi carp.

And they were not going to have any of mine!

A skilful grey heron in action

My mate Pete, the speedy 'brickie' and me as his labourer, completed the job in two days. On my own, it would have taken two weeks.

Although I was eager to fill the pond with water, I left it for seven days to make sure the concrete had gone off completely and no residue from the cement would pollute the water.

In the meantime, I installed a filter system and connected it to a powerful pump that was going to circulate and oxygenate the water, plus an ornamental fountain.

Boy, was this going to look grand, or what?

I didn't half spoil those cats or was it me being

spoilt? I just hoped that when the pond was finished, those furry guests would appreciate it. Meaning all my hard work.

Using a shovel and rake, I covered the pipework and filter with a lorry load of fine pea gravel. Then I spread another load of gravel that was almost as big as hen eggs. What a challenge that was on such a hot day.

Eventually, the exciting long-awaited pond-filling day came. To fill the pond, I left a hosepipe running for twenty-four hours. I must say, when the water finally reached the top, it looked an absolute picture. Especially with the pump running with the fountain cascading. I was advised to wait thirty days before I stocked the pond with fish so that the water could settle and any impurities from the building work would have been filtered out.

The very next morning, after the pond filling, I had a big surprise. And it was not a nice one! Contented with all the hard work, I stood on the landing and looked through the window. My contentment didn't last many seconds, because I was more than shocked to see a heron standing patiently by our beautiful new pond. The heron was probably wondering when my fish were arriving. Was this tall, lanky bird a clairvoyant, or what? I knew these guys were intelligent predators, but I sure as heck didn't expect them to find my isolated tranquil pond that quickly.

I knew exactly where the waiting heron had come from. There was a large heronry at Aqualate Mere, which is a large stretch of water about four miles away as the crow flies, or should I say has the heron flies.

I decided there and then, the hungry bird was not having any of my fish.

No, I didn't shoot it!

Don't forget, I am a conservationist.

I decided to rig up a permanent fence of black nylon netting around the edge of the pond. The height of the net was two feet. Not only was it going to protect my lovely fish from the herons, it was also protection to stop small children from falling into the water when they were visiting the cattery with their parents. Initially, I thought the black netting was going to spoil the look of the pond, but it didn't stand out at all, in fact, it looked quite camouflaged.

At long last, it was time to introduce the fish. My excitement was building with the anticipation of Koi carp cruising around the beautiful new pond.

Our very good friend Neville, who happens to be the star of the following chapter, kindly drove Kathy and me, with his wife Paula to a village called Lawton, near Stoke-on-Trent. We rode in style in his posh Daimler Jaguar, to a retailer who specialised in Koi carp that Neville had recommended. As we walked around the holding tanks we deliberated and chose twelve Koi carp of various colours and sizes.

When the fish were delivered by the retailer, they were released into the water by Neville and me as Kathy and Paula watched on. The twelve Koi carp took to their new environment like 'Ducks to Water', or in this case... 'Fish to Water'.

After all the hard work involved, I was so proud of the finished product, our new Koi carp pond.

This was our advert in Yellow Pages.

OUR FELINE GUESTS CAN GAZE FROM THEIR LUXURIOUS QUARTERS AT THE EXOTIC KOI CARP BASKING IN THEIR BEAUTIFUL ORNAMENTAL POND

No cat in its right mind would be able to refuse a stay with us after reading that advert. But maybe it was the owners that read the advert. It sounded just like feline paradise!

SO PARADISE, IT WAS GOING TO BE!

Kathy bought me a posh wooden bench as a celebration that doubled as a future birthday present. I placed the bench facing the cattery building so that in the evenings with a drink in our hands we could amuse ourselves watching the cruising carp and the antics of the cats.

When my birthday arrived, as a surprise Kathy bought me two very large, expensive Koi carp. One was gold and the other was a metallic silvery-white colour. And it took me hours of racking my brains to come up with the unique names of Goldie and Silver.

Well, maybe only seconds!

Goldie and Silver were the stars of the pond, and also the giants, they were about eighteen inches long. We used to love sitting on the birthday bench watching them effortlessly glide through the water. After a year, the two fish virtually doubled in weight and became very bold, or should I say tame. When it was feeding time, they glided sedately over to me and took food gently from my hand making a relaxing sucking and gurgling sound.

I am not sure who got the most pleasure from the pond with the fountain, water lilies and basking fish. The patiently watching cats, or me!

But...

Here comes some stress...

One evening, Kathy and I went out for a meal to a local pub/restaurant with my mother, Irene, sister Gail and her partner Dave. On arriving back at our cottage at around 11 pm, Gail and Dave walked over to admire the pond fifty yards away from our garden gate.

As I was unlocking the front door, Gail shouted in a panicky tone,

“GEOFF! Come here quick, a big fish is lying on the grass."

Knowing my little sister, I thought it was a joke and chose to ignore her and entered the front door of the cottage. I knew Gail would come in shortly because she would soon get bored waiting for me.

In the meantime, Kathy had gone back out to Gail and the next thing I heard was Kathy shouting,

"GEOFF! GEOFF! Come quick! Honestly, she's not joking!"

I thought,

'Ha, ha, my little sister has got my mischievous wife playing along with her now.'

But my curiosity got the better of me, so I went out into the darkness, only to find to my horror...

She hadn't been joking at all!

Because...

Sadly...

Lying on the lawn...

Was my lovely Silver!

My silvery-white birthday present lying lifelessly on its side only a yard or so from the pond.

'OH, NO!!!'

Then Gail got my hopes up,

She said,

“I think it is still alive.”

And, sure enough, it was!

With that, I wetted my hands in the pond then gently picked up the gasping fish from the damp grass and carefully lowered it back into the water. After suspending it in the water for a while, I could feel it getting stronger and stronger. Suddenly, with a flick of its tail, the handsome fish swam slowly away, fortunately looking none the worse for its ordeal.

Unbelievingly, it was obvious that Silver had leapt clean over my two-foot-high heron security fence.

Didn't Silver realise he was a Koi carp, not a leaping salmon!

So that was the moment I realised my very first job in the morning would be to raise the height of the heron fence.

When my mother, Gail and Dave left, I went over to the pond to make sure we had no more wannabe salmon.

During that night, I was very restless dreaming about, fish, fishing and leaping salmon. I went outside more than once during that night, to make sure my big silver fish hadn't done another repeat performance.

Having feared the worst when I had first spotted Silver, I couldn't believe the miracle. Yes, it was a miracle, because if we hadn't been out that evening with my family and they hadn't come back for coffee, that poor beautiful fish would most certainly have been lying dead by the pool the next morning and probably half-eaten by a greedy heron, to boot.

It was early summer and I reckoned the reason Silver leapt out of the water, was probably because it was the mating season for carp.

Apparently, fish mating ceremonies take place like this and my Silver obviously preferred it with the lights off. I later found out that in the fish world, it is the males that do all the chasing and leaping.

Could this be similar to our human world?

Sod's law, out of all the fish in the pond, it had to be my favourite and the biggest that tried to commit suicide.

Why do traumas always happen, to something you treasure most?

This fishy story gets better...

Our fourteen fish didn't remain fourteen in number for long, because they bred like randy rabbits. Their nightly jaunts proved to have been very successful in production terms and fortunately, they didn't do any more night-time flying.

One year later, after the mating ceremonies

had commenced, the fish had multiplied from fourteen to fourteen hundred and that was no exaggeration. Other than my lovely Silver being a male, I had no idea how many of the others were females or males. But as we all know you only need one male to make things happen in the breeding world.

When I built my pond, I had aimed to have fourteen fish swimming around, not one thousand four hundred. Anyway, the little fry soon grew to the size of my index finger. Every morning when I put in my appearance to feed them, they headed for me so fast they created a mini bow wave.

'What on earth am I going to do with all these fish? At the rate they are breeding, I will soon be able to walk across the pond on their backs!'

With those thoughts, I could have given a good impression of that famous man from the Bible who walked on water.

A friend informed me of a lady who lived near Stafford. Apparently, she owned a nursing home with a large ornamental pond in its grounds and she wanted to stock it with fish. So I gave her a ring and she was only too pleased to take some fish from my hands, and as a bonus, she offered me two hundred pounds for my trouble. I assured her, thinking about the two hundred pounds, it would be no trouble at all. By then, I was thinking in terms of commercial fish farming as it appeared to be so easy.

But how was I going to catch all these fish?

Well, it was not long before I came up with an idea of a nylon net fixed to a square aluminium frame. The frame would measure 4 x 4 feet square, with a long 6-foot handle. I had the frame and handle made up by a local welder and then I attached the black nylon fish netting to it.

I placed my new contraption in the water just below the surface. All I had to do was to entice the multitudes of fish over the top of the net and then yank it quickly up in the air and swing it away from the pond.

Easy!

BUT, HOW WRONG CAN ONE BE?

Later that day, I threw the fish food in at the usual time and I just couldn't believe what my eyes were witnessing. Even though the fish were really hungry, the normally brazen little devils just didn't want to know. They just would not go anywhere near that darned net.

Did someone say fish have no brains, well my fish sure had, and I think they talked to each other as well.

So where do we go from here?

How do I outwit those fishy Einsteins?

Pitting my wits against them, I cunningly formed a devious plan.

I decided to lower the net to the bottom of the pond and gradually bring it up a little higher each day just after they had been fed. So, with the net six feet below the surface, I decided to leave it there for a few days.

Perhaps this would do the trick.

And yes, it worked.

Because the large shoal of hungry fingerling fish fed in their usual frenzy on the surface, well above the sunken net.

It takes more than the brains of a few hundred fish to outwit me!!!

So, as each day passed, gradually, I raised the net closer to the surface. After ten days it was only three inches below the feeding fish. The day I proposed to net the fish was looming up fast and it was looking very much like I was in for a really big catch. I decided when I had caught most of the large shoal of fish I would transport them in six old aluminium milk churns. In years gone by churns were used to transport milk, 11 imperial gallons (50 litres).

Previously, I had used the milk churns in my game-keeping days, to transport water for the pheasants to various dry parts of the Country Estate.

Kathy, being a farmer's daughter, remembers her grandad using churns to store milk from the hand-milked cows. The milk-filled churns stood in a cool building and were kept cool by running cold water down the outside. They stood there until they were loaded onto a tractor and trailer and then driven to the bottom of the drive where they were collected by the milk lorry to be pasteurised and bottled.

Milk Churn Facts

In the United Kingdom and other European

countries, milk churns were left by dairy farmers by the roadside on purpose-built platforms, or stands, at the right height to be loaded on to the dairy's cart or lorry. They fell out of use when milk began to be collected by tanker from the farm and ceased entirely by 1979. Some stands remain in the countryside as historical features, but most have been dismantled or left to decay.

Milk Churns

Ok, back to the fish...

The big day arrived.

I parked my Daihatsu 4 x 4 containing the milk churns next to the pond and three-quarter filled them up with pond water. The fish were in their usual feeding frenzy splashing over the net. I was looking forward to this! Holding the long handle of the net with both hands I waited for the right moment. And it came. Suddenly, I whipped the net right out of the water. Lo and behold, there were so many glistening silver and gold fish trapped in the net I only just had enough strength to lift and swing it out onto the grass. Kathy was waiting to help count them into the milk churns. Carefully and patiently, we counted just over two hundred of the wriggling little chaps into the old churns.

Not bad for the first day's catch!

So, off we journeyed to Stafford to release them into their newfound home. And as a bonus, I was going to pick up two hundred pounds for my troubles.

The next day, when the fish feeding time arrived, to my dismay, none of the remaining little varmints wanted to know, they gave me the fishy cold shoulder.

I had heard in the past that some eminent scientist had proclaimed fish have only got a memory of seven seconds.

Well, all I can say is,

"Whoever you are, you have never been more wrong mate."

My super-intelligent fish took three weeks before they would feed over that net again.

Throughout that year, I spent a tremendous amount of time and effort trying to outwit those so-called brainless fish. Eventually, I reduced their numbers to less than a hundred. I never sold anymore, I just gave them away to friends, who had small garden ponds. And hopefully, not to feed the local herons!

Our very good friends for many years, Rick and Bet, whom I mentioned in a hilarious story in my first book, had recently moved house. In the grounds, they had a very large natural pond. It was situated at the bottom of their garden and was full of rare yellow water lilies. That year, I took hundreds of the little fish over to that lovely pond.

The question was,

"Would I have this problem with my sexy fish breeding like this every year?"

Perhaps I needed to get them on some form of birth control for the years to come.

NOW HERE COMES THE STRESSFUL PART OF THE STORY...

One cold winter's morning I had a bit of a fright. Actually, a massive fright would be a more appropriate description.

It was a very frosty morning when Kathy looked out of our upstairs landing window, which overlooked the grounds of the cattery and kennels, and of course, our beautiful Koi carp pond.

Kathy screamed out,

"GEOFF! GEOFF! Come here quick! Look at this!"

'Here we go again!'

I rushed out of the bedroom to join her at the landing window. I half expected to see some rare bird or animal.

But no!

No such luck!

WHAT I SAW FILLED ME WITH ABSOLUTE DREAD.

The Koi carp pond and the immediate area looked like...

ICE CITY!

Overnight, some phenomenon created a beautiful spectacle of ice. It looked like an intricate carving which expanded at least thirty feet around the Koi carp pond in all directions. Everything in that area looked to be frozen solid. Adding a polar bear to the scene would not have been out of place.

Kathy gasped in horror,

"Oh no! All the fish must be dead! How can they still be alive in that frozen water?"

She must have been reading my mind.

Well, that wouldn't have taken much!

We ran outside to inspect the tragedy, and to my utmost relief, it wasn't quite the tragedy I had envisaged.

The level of the pond had dropped by three feet, so the shallowest part of the pond was completely empty. But luckily, the bottom level still had a depth of three feet of water, which is exactly where all the fish had safely congregated.

PHEW! THANK GOODNESS FOR THAT!

Those fish had even got the brains and sense to save themselves, unlike the super-intelligent whales that at times beach themselves in large numbers, therefore committing mass suicide.

I quickly found the problem.

Due to the very severe hoarfrost, the return pipe from the pump which was situated on the upper level had burst a joint and with the pump still running, it completely emptied the top level by squirting the precious water here there and everywhere across the surrounding lawn.

Thank goodness the filters were only at the highest level, or we would have lost all the water.

And much worse, all of the fish.

Did somebody once tell me that keeping a Koi carp pond was a tranquil occupation?

Well on that day, the person who came up with that one, should have changed places with me!

Over the years, we had a tremendous amount of pleasure out of the pond and lots of fun with our fishing escapades.

I am sure that the cats with the view enjoyed it too.

CHAPTER 12

My Friend Neville

This guy is unstoppable.

Originally, we met Neville through our business, but initially, I dealt mostly with his wife Paula who used to bring their Airedale dog Bruce to board with us.

Bruce had a very nice character and was easy to look after, which was a good job, because he came in many times a year, mostly at weekends.

I developed my friendship with Neville through a mutual hobby, keeping Koi carp, which you will have learned in the last story.

When Kathy and I retired and moved to Spain, Neville and Paula followed in our footsteps and resided only twenty minutes away from where we lived.

Now Neville could spin many a yarn. And he was very good at it too.

I suppose it was because of his history of being a salesman, which led him to own his own company. He must have been very good at selling, especially with him able to retire early.

So, over the years we had many dinners with Neville and his lovely wife Paula.

Hopefully, after Neville reads this story, that trend will continue!

When Nev, I am getting friendly now by shortening his name, I could even be creeping, told his stories around the dinner table, he was extremely explicit.

I always joked that Neville could pick up an

empty clear-glass bottle and talk about it for half an hour, when most of us being much less gifted, would only be able to talk about it for a half second!

If Neville was interrupted in full entertaining flow by Paula in her enthusiasm to help him tell his long, long-lasting story quicker, he banged the palm of his hand on the table with a loud boom and looking into his beloved one's eyes said,

"Who's telling this story? You! Or me?"

I have to say, we felt for Paula because she looked dejected and embarrassed.

With that, Neville continued on his way with his ultra-long story which we had all heard so many, many times before.

BORING US ALL TO DEATH!

Inevitably, at dinner parties, I have noticed that sometime during the evening, someone will talk about their pet or pets.

And Neville was no exception!

Neville loved Bruce very much, and he most

certainly narrated plenty of stories about him.

Neville's favourite story was about how he and Paula went to the Airedale breeder to choose a puppy. Now Neville was more explicit in this story than in any other story he ever recited.

Neville's three-minute story could easily take the best part of half an hour. It was a very nice story, but unfortunately, one I had heard about four thousand times before. Well, I suppose that is a slight exaggeration, three thousand nine hundred and ninety-nine would perhaps be a little nearer the mark!

So by now, I most certainly knew every word about the discovery of Bruce, off by heart.

One very memorable evening Neville, with more than enough Spanish wine inside him, started the same old story yet again around our dinner table. We were sitting with our mutual friends Bob and Diana who had heard this particular story several times before, but nothing like the number of times we had, believe me! And it looked like nothing was going to stop Neville, from boring us to death...

Yet again!

Neville was fifteen minutes into his story and I was starting to get a bit twitchy, or even slightly agitated...

Because I knew there was at least another fifteen minutes to go!

'*ARGHHH!*'

So I did...

The unthinkable!

I interrupted him.

I stood up, banged the palm of my hand on the table. Just like Neville had done so many times with Paula in the past.

It stopped him...

Absolutely, dead...

In his tracks...

The room went deadly silent...

He looked up at me, in absolute amazement.

This was probably the first time anybody had dared interrupt him, especially when he was in full flow.

Nervously, and unable to assess what on earth was coming, I laughed out loud and said,

"Nev let me tell you what happens next."

He stared at me with his jaw dropped open. He was moving his mouth, but no words were coming out. I have to say this was unusual for our Neville, or should I say, even a miracle!

I continued his story, with a big grin on my face,

"Bruce walked toward me with his tail between his little legs and I knew this was the pup for me."

Neville looked at me like I was some sort of magician and said,

"How on earth did you know that?"

I ignored him as I continued with a big grin on my face, to accurately tell more of the story which happened on that first day when he met Bruce.

Everyone burst into laughter, including my friend Neville.

Since that day, we have never, heard that story again.

After all, we didn't need to, we knew it off by heart!

CHAPTER 13

Evil Eyes

An exciting fast-moving story.

With this story, we have moved quite a few years down the road from the start of the business.

It was early March and I had been extending the size of the cattery. In fact, I was doubling the size of the building. Most of the construction was over and the only work remaining was inside the cattery.

It was a lovely spring morning and I decided to do a bit of tidying up. Some excess building materials were scattered about in a small area of the bordering woodland. My untidiness comprised of roofing sheets, building blocks and bricks. My intention was to stack them into a compact pile for future use. Most of it had been scattered around for three months or so. It was out of the view of the public eye; therefore, I had not been in too much of a hurry to shift it. I had been too busy building and now I had time to tidy it up before it got enveloped by woodland undergrowth. By habit, I am a tidy person and I hate to see anything out of place. Meticulously, I pick up any offending rubbish, especially cigarette butts, which I personally hate with venom, probably because I have never smoked.

Just a point of interest, I once read that it takes thirty-five years for a cigarette butt to decompose.

My way of thinking is, if customers could see rubbish lying around our premises, what sort of mess was inside, where their pets were boarded.

I was quite relishing the project of tidying up. I calculated it would take me close to four hours to complete. I waded into the work with great enthusiasm as I always did with a new task.

After three hours I had removed all the blocks and bricks with my trusty wheelbarrow and all that remained were half a dozen off-white corrugated roofing sheets. Although the 10 x 3 feet corrugated sheets were quite big, with them being quite light they were not too much of a problem for a single person to lift.

After removing and stacking five of the sheets, it was the turn of sheet number six.

But…

Before I started to lift it, I noticed with

my trained gamekeeper's eye something that disturbed me...

The grass had been worn away forming a path that led under the sheet.

MY ALARM BELLS STARTED TO RING!!!

Slowly and very carefully I raised the sheet just a few inches off the ground.

Sure enough, my suspicions were well-founded!

As I peered warily under the sheet into the darkness, I wasn't the slightest bit surprised...

To see...

Five pairs of slanted eyes...

Glaring back at me...

RATS!!!

Yes, they were rats. Young rats, five of the germ-carrying pests. Carefully I lowered the sheet, so as not to disturb them. Stealthily I backed away whilst keeping my eyes fixed on the entrance under the sheet making sure that they remained underneath.

Nothing moved!

'Good, I'll sort you boys out in a minute.'

On numerous occasions in my gamekeeping past I have had to deal with the problem of rats, and I am sorry, but those five young rats had to go. In other words, die!!! For sure, I could not take the risk of letting them multiply in our landscaped grounds.

Fact

Rats will breed all the year-round, providing there is food in the vicinity. The alarming thing is that rats reach maturity after nine weeks. This means that a population can grow in one year from 2 to 1,250, with the potential to grow exponentially. The UK population of humans is 68 million.

Rats exceed 150 million!!!

'ARGHHH!'

Most people do not realise that most of the population in the United Kingdom live within thirty feet of a rat.

'ARGHHH!'

So tonight, make sure your toilet lid is down. Rats can use this route to infiltrate a house directly from the stinking sewers.

'ARGHHH!'

So after that little piece of scintillating information, I am sure that now you do not mind if I get on with exterminating those cuddly rats. Well Kathy like a lot of people would not call them cuddly, she hates rats with venom and is literally scared to death of them. With their long horrible tails, pointed faces and yellow teeth. (Kathy's description.)

So, how was I going to do this absolutely necessary deed?

Well, I could have fetched a stick and knocked them on the head.

But no, rats are very fast, so I would have been lucky if I got one of them as they dispersed in all directions.

To me, the obvious solution to get rid of the pests was, to get out the gun and ammo, meaning my double-barrelled 12-bore shotgun. In previous times, my trusty gun had sorted out dozens of rats.

On this occasion, I was going to need help from one of my brave girls.

Well, I couldn't ask Kathy, because as brave as she is with most things, unfortunately, she is absolutely terrified of mice, let alone rats. And I mean over-the-top terrified!

So it was a definite no-go area for her.

Conveniently, the girls were having their mid-morning break in the staff room. So that was an ideal time for me to ask for a willing volunteer.

I popped my head through the door and said,

"Is there anyone here, who isn't frightened of rats?"

There were six girls in there and they looked at me in amazement, almost as if I was an alien. Maybe they thought I was going to ask them to start looking after pet rats as well as cats and dogs.

One brave girl Charlotte answered suspiciously,

"I'm not. Why?"

"Well, I've got a little job I want you to help me with."

She was very apprehensive,

"What are you getting me into now Geoff?"

"Don't you worry, come with me and I'll show

you."

So off we went, and as we were walking across the lawn to where the little horrors were lurking, I explained to her why and how the young rats, unfortunately, had to die.

I explained my plan,

"All I want you to do is lift up the roofing sheet very quickly and flick it away from you. Then step back to the left moving as fast as you can with your hands pressed over your ears. I will be twenty feet or so behind you diagonally to your right."

Charlotte was concerned!

"Why, do I need my hands over my ears?"

"The rats aren't going to try and get into my, ears are they?"

I laughed.

"No! But have you ever been close to a shotgun when it goes off?"

"No!"

"Well, it makes a big, big bang, which could damage your ears!"

I showed her my ear protectors which I would be wearing. Also, I informed her that I had shot a tremendous amount of twelve-bore cartridges before the age of twenty-one, unfortunately without ear protectors. Hence, I have lost some of my upper level of hearing, and I most certainly did not want to damage Charlotte's ears.

I am right-handed, which means the butt of the gun comes up rapidly against my right shoulder. This automatically lines the sighting of the rib that runs between the gun barrels to my right master eye. When aiming a rifle you close one eye, but with a shotgun, you keep both eyes open. And that, my friends, is how you aim a shotgun.

Being slightly deaf can be very handy, especially when Kathy wants me to do something. Sometimes I pretend not to hear her, I am only joking! This is known as selective hearing. But seriously I would much rather have complete hearing, especially because I cannot hear a lot of high-pitched beautiful bird songs and other nice sounds, such as a quiet babbling brook.

Anyway, back to the rats.

We almost got to the spot where all the action was about to take place.

My dubious helper whispered,

“What if the rats run at me?”

“They won’t. Trust me.”

Gingerly, Charlotte crept forward and I could see trepidation in her every step.

I loaded both barrels of the shotgun, closed the gun with a metallic click and let off the safety catch by pushing it forward with my right thumb.

Also, I had two more cartridges in my left hand that would be supporting the barrels as I swung the gun. I needed the spare cartridges ready to reload quickly because if I missed with the first two barrels, the targets, once they had been exposed were going to bolt out in different directions.

My plan was to try and kill all five rats with one shot before they even got a chance to move. I would be standing about twenty feet away from the nest of rats. Therefore, there would be an ample spread of lead pellets from the shotgun to take out all five rats with one shot. Then I would have three cartridges spare for emergencies, plus four more cartridges in my pocket.

Charlotte, my brave young helper was all set to go into action.

In my position of readiness to Charlotte's right, I gave her the nod, she bent down quickly and flicked over the roofing sheet that revealed five half-grown rats.

But to her horror...

There was an enormous sixth rat...

THE DOE RAT!

The mother of the five smaller rats.

Brave Charlotte...

SCREAMED!!!

As instructed, Charlotte backed away rapidly to my left, putting her diagonally across and slightly behind me.

I fired the right barrel.

BANG!!!

Charlotte... SCREAMED!!!

The mother rat was quick!

Too quick!

She dived out...

Off to my right.

Four offspring were dead.

The surviving young rat sped directly away from me.

I swung the second barrel through the doe rat.

A diagonal crossing shot to my right.

I pulled the trigger.

BANG!!!

Charlotte...SCREAMED!!!

The cunning doe rat cartwheeled over.

Stone-dead!

Thirty feet away.

The sole survivor was still running.

Rapidly, I flicked the top lever across with my right thumb...

Dropping the gun barrels open.

This action automatically ejected the spent cartridge over my right shoulder.

In a split second...

I reloaded the empty chambers.

I snapped the gun shut.

In the same smooth motion...

I swung through the speeding....

Last target...

BANG!!!

Brave Charlotte...SCREAMED!!!

The last rat was dead!

'Well, that's sorted that little problem!'

All the action took place in less than five seconds. After the rapid firing ceased, the silence was almost deafening.

As I ejected the third spent shell into my left hand. I could smell the familiar odour of cordite floating in the air.

With no more rats in sight, I removed the remaining fourth live shell from the chamber of the gun and put it back in my pocket.

My excited helper exclaimed,

"Wow, that's the last thing I would have expected to see today, a cowboy shootout. You've just shot six rats in less than ten seconds!"

"Probably less than five!" Was my cool reply.

"Well, you'll be the first person I'll get my dad to ring up if we have burglars."

"Well, yes, I suppose burglars are just another type of rat."

For a while, after that very memorable incident, the staff joked and called me Clint after the famous gun-toting movie star. Clint Eastwood.

And hey, I didn't mind one little bit.

It felt quite an honour.

CHAPTER 14

Human Rats

Human rats, is a very appropriate title after that exciting cowboy story.

So, here comes the two-legged variety…

Humans!

Generally running a business like ours was fun, but in any business, there will always be a serious side that has to be faced and you have to stand up for yourself, especially when it involves money. As the saying goes, 'People get funny when it comes to money'.

So what are human rats?

In my opinion, one type of human rat is the kind that we have experienced defaulting a payment after their pets stay. They write us a cheque that is rejected by their bank, better known as 'A bouncing cheque'. Today, very few people use cheques, it is usually bank transfers or plastic cards.

Now some people bounce cheques by accident, maybe because they have not monitored their bank accounts correctly and mistakenly issued a cheque from an account where there are not enough funds to cover it, therefore it bounces.

Meaning it is returned unpaid.

A funny word isn't it, 'bouncing cheque'. What always springs to my mind is a bouncing ball, not a 'bouncing cheque', they don't seem to go together somehow.

But then you have that other kind of person, the human rat that knowingly does it on purpose.

They write out a cheque knowing full well that it is going to 'bounce'!

Our policy was, no one, and I mean no one, was allowed to collect their pet until they had paid first.

This rule made us pretty safe from having to chase bills, that would have been both time-consuming and expensive. Luckily, ninety-nine point nine per cent of all our customers were downright honest and really appreciated how we looked after their pets.

But there is always a minority...

We had been in business for about a year and were doing quite nicely, thank you very much, when the very first customer's cheque bounced. I will always remember the amount; it was only a small sum of £21.25. Sometimes small is beautiful, but certainly not in this case. Anyway, it was the principle that mattered to me. I wouldn't have done that to anyone, so why should anyone do it to me, especially if they were satisfied with the service they had received, so surely, they should be honest with their payment.

AND HERE COMES THE FIRST RAT!

I had dealt with this guy personally and at the time he seemed to be quite a nice person. I knew he was pleased with his dog the day he collected it. Perhaps he had made a mistake with the 'bouncing cheque'. So, I decided to ring him up using his works number that was on his dog booking form. I dialed the number. The call was answered immediately by a lady, possibly his secretary.

I asked her if it was possible to speak to the gentleman concerned. She asked me who I was, and I told her. I could hear whispering on the other end of the line.

After a few seconds, she said,

"I'm sorry, but he's out."

I replied,

"Can you please ask him to phone me when he gets back?"

And guess what?

He never returned my call!

I phoned his business number on many occasions over the following weeks and I always got the same reply,

"I'm sorry, but he's out!"

I never did believe her reply.

Eventually, through a friend in business, I learned that the rat's company was in financial trouble, so I decided to make one last call and the reply yet again was,

"I'm sorry, but he's out."

I said to the lady very coolly,

"Do you realise your boss owes me money and his business is going down the pan?"

With that short, sharp sentence I hung up.

Within minutes, the man himself rang me back, he yelled down the phone,

"Do you realise what you've just done?"

"YOU IDIOT!"

"No. What?"

He snarled,

"You have just frightened all my staff to death. They think they're all going to lose their jobs."

By the sound of his tone, I could tell he was in a vile temper.

I said to him in a very professional manner,

"If you hadn't avoided all my phone calls and paid me the money you owe me, this would never have happened. So can you please pay me the £21.25 you owe me?"

And this is what he said,

"IF YOU CALL ME ONCE MORE, I'LL COME OVER THERE AND BREAK BOTH YOUR LEGS!"

Well, he was more explicit with his words, but they are not for this book!

He slammed down the phone.

I just couldn't believe what I had just heard. There was a crooked man, who owed me money...

AND HE WAS THREATENING ME WITH VIOLENCE!

Hey, if he had known how handy I was with a shotgun, he might not have said that to me.

It was only out of principle, that I put the matter in the hands of my solicitor Mike, who I made famous in a hilarious story in the first book of this series.

Well, I never did get my £21.25, it was my first debt that I had to write off, so for sure, that particular customer was a real rotten human rat. Fortunately, he never came to break my legs. For sure, I did not want to be in a situation where I would have had to shoot the big rotten rat as I tried to defend my poor little legs.

Ginny

The next cheque bouncer was a very nice lady. Well, she seemed to be, initially!

She owned a lovely-natured Rottweiler bitch named Ginny and it appeared that Ginny was going to be with us for a long time. Ginny's owner was unsure just how long it would be. So, the deal agreed was that she was going to pay us monthly.

The first monthly cheque came in and went through the banking system with no problems at all. It was the second one that bounced and each week Ginny's owner asked me to present the cheque again as funds would be there. But each time it bounced! As the weeks passed into the next month, Ginny's owner over the phone informed me that the next cheque would be for two months payment.

She assured me that the next cheque would be

okay.

'OH NO!'

That cheque bounced as well!

This continued for some months and it wasn't long before poor Ginny had run up a bill with us for over £600.00, which was an awful lot of money in those days.

I was in constant touch with Ginny's owner, enduring long telephone conversations, but alas, no money was forthcoming, just false promises from the lady who was previously so nice.

By then, she had become a member of the lying human rat club.

Finally, I had enough of the nagging situation and decided to take Ginny back to her owner. As much as we loved having Ginny, we were not a charity. It just was not possible to run a successful business that way, we were a boarding kennel, not a rescue home for dogs.

With a little investigation, I found out that Ginny's owner was running a small manufacturing business in Telford. A proper little detective I had become, especially if it concerned some human rat owing us money.

It was a mid-Monday morning when I walked through her small factory door with gentle Ginny at my side.

Ginny appeared to be a great big fearsome-looking brute of a Rottweiler. Of course, she was not fearsome at all. She just looked it. Actually, she was as soft as the proverbial brush.

The astonished staff (over a dozen) stared at me in amazement. And in some cases, maybe in fear. Not of me, but of the big Rottweiler walking by my side. Ginny's owner who wasn't exactly too pleased to see me, with a look of shock on her face, rushed over to me and ushered me outside, pleading with me to give her more time to pay.

I was having none of it!

I knew if I took Ginny back to our kennels, I was going to be in the same situation, just running up an even higher bill with her fake promises. She wanted to give me yet another cheque which I wouldn't accept. It would have been over my dead body!

Believe me, by then, I had enough rubber cheques from Ginny's owner to make a mattress for a bed.

Finally, after a heated discussion, we ended up going down to her bank there and then, with Ginny in tow and I got paid by cash in full.

After paying me, Ginny's owner pleaded with me to take her back to our kennels, but I told her unless she paid me in advance, in cash, I was not having Ginny back.

So, that was the end of our relationship with Ginny, who had up until then, been our longest-staying guest.

Goldy

Printed at the bottom, in bold print on both cat and dog booking forms was...

ANIMALS NOT COLLECTED WITHIN TWO WEEKS OF THE AGREED COLLECTION DATE WILL BE DISPOSED OF AT OUR DISCRETION.

Now that statement certainly rattled a few cages,

I can tell you!

Actually, it was a warning to callous people who just wanted to dump their unwanted pets on us and never return. Its true meaning was, if their cat or dog was not collected within a reasonable time of the date agreed, we would not be responsible for them. So, any owners that really loved their pets and fully intended to collect them had absolutely nothing to fear at all. Before they completed their booking form, we did have a few concerned caring customers ring up to find out what that statement really meant. When we fully explained it to them, it put them totally at ease.

Being an animal lover myself, if the owner did not turn up, I was hardly going to drag a protesting cat or dog out of the building, take it into the wood and cold-bloodedly shoot it. Was I? But, I suppose the caring owner was afraid of what I might do because for sure, they didn't even know me. Those words 'disposed of' do have a bit of a mysterious ring to them.

One day, I had an American lady ring up and book a kennel for her Golden Retriever named Goldy. Yes, yet another Goldy. Along with Goldy came two cats, so we would be looking after a family of three.

The lady owner explained to me over the phone that her three pets were going to stay with us for about a month because she was going to join her husband in America. Allegedly, he was setting up a large company and was going to make loads and loads of lovely money. Well, I've heard that one before, but her story did seem quite genuine.

We arranged that she would pay a month in advance and initially, she did, with no problem at all. The plan was, she would send for her family of three when things had been settled across the Atlantic. Then I was going to arrange for them to be transported to America.

If the three pets were likely to be with us for any longer than the month, she was going to authorise another payment in advance through her accountant, and she gave me his telephone number. So, there was never going to be any problem with the money side of things...

Or so I thought!

Anyway, so far, so good, the story she had given me sounded as if nothing could go wrong.

HERE WE GO AGAIN!

Goldy and her two feline friends settled in very quickly and the staff grew to love them just as if they were their own. The month passed by very quickly and during that period the lady owner rang up several times, to see how the three were getting on.

On the very last phone call I received from her, she said,

"I'm afraid things are taking a little longer than we anticipated here in America. I will need to extend their stay and I will arrange for the next payment to be sent to you."

Well, that sounded like no problem.

No problem, at all!

Her three pets were very easy to look after and if all the animals were like those three, we could think we were in a pet hotel paradise. But we weren't, were we? Because to cap it all, we received no more money!

This owner had become an American human rat, joining the British human rat club.

I rang up the owner's accountant several times

and he kept assuring me that everything was running smoothly in America. And anyway, the people were so wealthy they virtually had money sprouting out of their ears.

So, I had nothing to worry about...

Did I?

Another month fled by, but still no money and then three months passed by with no sign of any money forthcoming.

Whatever happened to those two words?

DISPOSE OF!

In the end, the accountant lost contact with the two so-called caring owners and we never saw any more money. Their bill was in the region of £3000.00. It was very sad and frustrating for us monetary wise. Well, 'You can't win em all', can you?

So, what did we decide to do with our three lovely friends?

Dispose of them?

No way!

Goldy was lucky because one of our girls Jenny fell in love with her and gave her a good home. As a bonus, Goldy spent many days with us, because she used to come to work with her new owner, Jenny.

We quickly found Goldy's two feline friends a new home, which fortunately kept the two of them happily together.

So, we did 'DISPOSE OF THEM' at our discretion after all!

We were quite fortunate because virtually all of our customers were not dirty human rats at all.

So as an extra bonus, there was no need to bring my shotgun out!

CHAPTER 15

My Signs

Okay, that's the serious stuff out of the way, so let's have some fun.

If anyone had informed me how many signs we needed to be displayed on our premises, I would never have believed the number.

SIGN 1

Believe it or not, we had to obtain planning permission for our very first sign. I erected it for all to see at the end of our drive on the wide grass verge that ran alongside the A41 highway.

CHETWYND FIRS CATTERY & KENNELS

And it was not there for long…

It was nicked by students!

SIGN 2

Here we go again!

CHETWYND FIRS CATTERY & KENNELS

Of course, sign one had to be replaced. Not only did it advertise our business, but it also made it easier for people to find our concealed entrance. I am quite sure it prevented numerous accidents as new customers drove slowly along the very fast highway searching for our concealed entrance hidden in the woodland.

I made doubly or should I say trebly sure that this one did not get nicked, I raised it high on scaffolding poles and concreted the bases in. Then I fastened the sign with nuts and bolts laced with super glue.

That cured that problem!

So, you mischievous drunken students, perhaps you now realise removing signs is not a good idea. It can be very, very dangerous.

SIGN 3

When we first started the business, we were open eighteen hours a day.

BIG, BIG MISTAKE!

We soon became quick learners and decided to have strict opening and closing times. The third sign simply read that we are closed and gave information about our opening times. I screwed it onto the new five-bar gate, situated along our drive fifty yards away from the car park serving the office.

CLOSED

HOURS 8 AM TO 5 PM

Unfortunately, the word closed didn't mean closed to a few persistent customers. They just ignored it and they had the audacity to open the gate and cruise through.

I soon cured that little problem with a very large padlock, but occasionally the brazen ones climbed over.

SIGN 4

So, I fixed a second sign on the gate, directly under the closed sign. In large bold BLOOD red capitals...

CLOSED

HOURS 8 AM TO 5 PM

DANGER GUARD DOGS LOOSE

This seemed to do the trick and that meant we were really, really closed.

It is a fact, that people in general do not like the idea of large vicious guard dogs running around loose.

But...

Not everyone took notice.

Some totally ignored it!

The guard dog sign was not a complete white lie, because we did have Sally, my more than friendly Springer Spaniel, she was always on the loose. But she preferred to lick people to death rather than show any aggression. I realise the wording seemed a bit dramatic, but when you have a business operating from home, you do have to have a break now and again. I am afraid some of the public seemed to think because we lived on the premises, we were there entirely for their convenience and whatever time they decided to drop in, we would be at their beck and call.

Can you believe a gentleman phoned us at 3 am one Sunday morning?

Yes, 3 am!

He wanted to book his two dogs in for the

following year.

'What?'

He was slurring his words, at least I managed to understand him because on the occasional Saturday night, after a hard day, I might have had one too many as well. Now that could have been some sort of amusing word-slurring conversation that could have been well worth listening to.

It was necessary to have the business line connected to the cottage so that we could at least pick up out-of-hours calls for what might have been a future booking. But surely not at that ridiculous hour. Also, hearing a phone ringing in the early hours can easily make one think that it is bad news regarding family. We definitely needed a second line connected to the office to get over the problem of the occasional way-out-of-hours call.

Only one line was down to our British telephone company B.T. In those days they had no serious competition and were notably a tadge slow at catering for the population's requests. A few years back, they advertised on TV using their famous yellow budgerigar 'Busby'. He was spouting on just how efficient they were. Apparently, 'Busby' could work wonders, except for installing Geoff's urgent second line. Eventually, 'Busby' installed it and we bought an answering machine. Problem sorted!

Anyway, enough of that, back to an amusing story involving the sign....

CLOSED
HOURS 8 AM TO 5 PM
DANGER GUARD DOGS LOOSE

One warm summer evening, I was sitting in the office concentrating on sorting out large piles of paperwork. This for me was the unfortunate side of my business because I most definitely preferred to be working outside. Well, as a consolation at least the office had a beautiful view.

It was just before nine o'clock in the evening and it was still quite light when I thought I heard a car engine and two doors slam.

'Ugh, ugh, what's going on here?'

I crept around my desk, slowly popped my head around the open door and looked out to my right through the bordering thin spinney of silver birch trees. The spinney which was about fifty yards deep separated the office and car park from the newly padlocked five-bar gate.

To my utter surprise and annoyance, and that is an understatement if ever I made one, there was a man and a woman climbing over the five-bar gate. They certainly didn't look like burglars…

They looked more like customers.

I just could not believe my eyes.

They had totally disregarded the two imposing signs.

Perhaps it should have read…

VERY DANGEROUS
GUARD DOGS LOOSE!!!

Or even…

YOU WILL GET RIPPED TO SHREDS AND
EATEN IF YOU MANAGE TO CLIMB
OVER THIS ELECTRIFIED GATE!!!

The couple, who appeared to be in their mid-fifties, were dressed respectfully and were creeping along the drive toward the car park. I could see they were quite wary, probably because they were imagining a pack of guard dogs loose. I knew they would not have been able to see the office clearly until they almost got to the car park. I must say I was more than annoyed with what I was witnessing. It was an evening of peaceful tranquility and I certainly did not want two brazen people entering our premises at this late hour. This blatant act would have undoubtedly disturbed the dogs resting or sleeping in the kennels. What I really mean is, I did not want the noise and bedlam to erupt with over one hundred hounds barking their heads off. No way was I going to let anybody, or anything, disturb that silent night.

As it turned out I wasn't needed…

Without any interference from me, nature took its course…

The intrepid couple were about to round the corner of the spinney when they hesitated and stopped. They were almost hidden from my view by small elderberry bushes growing in between the birches. The man pointed at something and I looked to see in what direction. To my utter amusement, he was pointing at the love of my life, Sally. She was on the grass not far from the office, curled up fast asleep with her back to them. From the distance they were looking, all they were able to see was a liver-coloured dog and they would not have been able to tell that Sally was a harmless twelve-year-old Springer

Spaniel.

Suddenly, Sally stirred and raised her head.

That was more than enough for the watching couple to contemplate.

They fled!

At speed, they bolted to the high five-bar gate which was no barrier to them whatsoever.

They virtually vaulted it!

Within seconds of their gymnastic manoeuvre, I heard car doors slamming, a car engine revving and tyres screeching. I must have had a huge grin on my face as I listened intently to the noise fading away as they sped down our twisting drive toward the A41 highway.

I burst out laughing and could only imagine what type of fierce guard dog they must have imagined my cuddly Sally to be. What made it so hilarious was that she was almost deaf and her sight was not too clever either. I patted my shin and beckoned her to come over. She looked at me with her faithful brown eyes, separated by her pretty white blaze. Faithfully, she trotted over with her liver-brown stumpy docked tail wagging away. I rolled her onto her back and tickled her white tummy. She must have wondered what on earth her master was laughing at.

Poor old Sally hadn't even realised the frightened couple had ever been there.

I have told this story many, many times around the dinner table and made friends laugh.

On that warm summer evening, if I really had a bit of devilment in me, I could have made it a lot more entertaining. I would have loved to have crept into the elderberry bushes to hide and wait for the moment the faltering couple spotted Sally. Then with perfect timing, I would have violently shaken the elder bushes and let out an almighty lion-like...

ROARRR!!!

I would bet my bottom dollar that despite their age, the couple would have cleared that five-bar gate in unison without even touching it. And more than likely they would have needed a change of underwear as well. Heaven forbids! I could have caused two major coronaries that evening.

Sally, the vicious guard dog!

SIGNS 5, 6, 7, 8, 9

The next signs were quite simple identifying different buildings, rooms, areas and so forth.

TOILET
CAR PARK
OFFICE
STAFF ROOM
KITCHEN

All quite self-explanatory.

Why would we need this next one you might ask?

SIGN 10

PRIVATE NO UNAUTHORISED CARS OR PEOPLE BEYOND THIS POINT

Why, because numerous customers just ignored the next sign with a pointing arrow.

SIGN 11

TO CAR PARK AND OFFICE

They just drove straight past the car park down to our peaceful cottage and knocked on the front door.

SIGN 12

Another sign, again straightforward enough...

NO UNAUTHORISED PERSONS TO OPEN THIS DOOR

This was fixed on the main security door to the first block of kennels. But some bright souls chose to ignore it and walked straight into the kennels. Because our canine guests did not recognise them as staff, the noise that erupted would make a jumbo jet seem quiet.

Why did customers ignore my beautiful signs?

What was it with these people?

Didn't they realise that entering a security door could lead to no end of problems?

I had to bite my tongue so often, but wow, did I get frustrated or what?

SIGN 13

This next sign caused all sorts of confusion. It was situated on the outside of the office wall, next to the main door for the first block of kennels...

PLEASE RING THE BELL FOR ATTENTION

There was a red arrow above the wording pointing toward a red button only two inches above. When the button was pressed it rang a loud buzzer in the first kennel block and of course, the dogs erupted into frenzied barking. In this block, there could be as many as thirty dogs. The barking started a chain reaction that spread to the other blocks. Wow, the noise that button created was unbelievable.

Simultaneously, a buzzer sounded in the cattery. Fortunately, the cats didn't mind it ringing. And as far as I know, no one has ever heard a cat bark!

The bell was necessary because the office could not be manned all the time, especially when dog walking. During this time, we needed, 'All hands-on deck'. It was inevitable that some dogs barked because their canine brains were not able to understand that they couldn't be walked at the same time.

We did our best to keep them as quiet as possible by taking the most excitable noisiest ones first. On their return, we shut them away in their sleeping quarters for the duration of the dog-walking session. If we heard a car coming up the drive, one of us would almost rupture a hernia trying to make an effort to get to the customer before he or she pressed that red button.

The office/reception was a room with a small window at the back with a view of all the runs inside kennel block one. We always left the office door open to encourage customers to look through the window so that they were able to see us working with the dogs. Then we could acknowledge them with a wave and mouth to them,

"We won't be a second."

But did they wait?

Of course,, they didn't!

They just had to press that button and start the dogs barking yet again.

We could be walking up from the cattery toward a customer standing outside the office. Even though we were in full view, and giving a cheery wave, on numerous occasions the customer acknowledged us with a cheery wave back but still pressed that button.

'ARGHHH!!!'

One day, I was standing outside the office talking to a customer and as I turned away, what did he do? To my utter astonishment, he pressed the red button and rang the buzzer.

I was stuck for words. What could I say?'

Occasionally, we had the impatient one who kept repeatedly pressing the red button.

I was astounded by how customers reacted to the

sign.

I joked with the staff,

"If anyone presses that button more than once, I'll get it wired up to have ten thousand volts passing through them!"

We used to ask people,

"Why did you press the button when you saw me coming toward you?"

"Well, the sign says 'Please ring' so I did."

'ARGHHH!!!'

I think once customers saw the sign that seemed to be the only sign they ever read, they just had to press that red button at all costs.

'I must press that button if it's the last thing I do!'

I was sure that if they were riddled with machine-gun bullets, they would still manage to drag their bleeding bodies across the car park, over to the sign and just manage to press that red button before they succumbed to their injuries. Wow, what stress that buzzer gave us and of course, it gave the dogs stress too. We had to find a way to solve the problem because that buzzer buzzing and the dogs barking that it automatically generated, was seriously getting right up my nose and certainly in my ears and of course, not forgetting the staff as well. For sure, before we all had nervous breakdowns, I needed to cure this irritating problem rapidly.

So, what could I do?

Out of the blue, a fantastic idea came to me.

What about replacing the annoying buzzer with a flashing light?

So, I did...

I drove down to the local builder's merchant in my home town Newport and purchased a flashing orange light. It was the same type tractors and diggers have on their cabs. I attached it to a high wooden stanchion I had fixed on top of the staffroom roof. This idea enabled us to see it from anywhere on the premises, even in the woodland as we were walking the dogs. So, when the dreaded red button was pressed, instead of the buzzer buzzing and creating the dog's frenzied barking, just the orange light flashed. So instantly, we knew someone needed our attention.

Ok, so we had a flashing light, but people could not hear a buzzer buzzing or a bell ringing.

So, what did they do?

They just simply kept pressing and pressing and pressing that red button that wasn't a problem anymore.

Because they thought it was not working.

'YES! YES! YES! MY IDEA WORKS!'

But we didn't mind anymore because the dogs didn't bark and pressing that lovely red button didn't get up my nose anymore.

Instead, it put a smile on my face!

So as far as I was concerned, they could press the button as much as they liked, and I have to confess, I was highly amused by that. And as the saying goes, 'There's more than one way to skin a cat'!

Numerous customers used to ask,

"Do you know your bell isn't working?"

We used to reply with a smile as we pointed to the flashing orange light in the sky, and say,

"Yes, but that is!"

They replied,

"Oh, what a wonderful idea."

Our famous flashing orange light was there for all to see and no dogs to hear.

Once the button had been pressed, all we had to do was press a hidden button in the office to switch the flashing orange light off.

Frequent customers got used to it.

Finally, tranquillity had arrived!

So why did we need this next sign? Oh yes, you will not believe this one!

SIGN 14

NO UNAUTHORISED PEOPLE

BEYOND THIS POINT PLEASE

One peaceful day with customers coming and going, the dogs in the second kennel block were going absolutely ballistic, it seemed for no apparent reason. I rushed to investigate the unbelievable disturbance. To my amazement, a strange man was wandering around the kennels staring at the dogs. The second block was well away from the office and no way would you think someone would have the cheek, or nerve to enter the kennels without our permission.

But that cheeky chap had!

As I approached him, I must have had a look of complete disbelief on my face and did an incredible job of controlling my spiralling temper.

With the customer always being right, I bit my tongue and said,

“I’m sorry, but you’re not meant to be in here. Can I help you?”

Nonchalantly, he replied,

“Oh, I’m just having a look around.”

Trying not to blow a gasket I asked,

"Didn't you see the large sign outside the kennel block?"

NO UNAUTHORISED PEOPLE

BEYOND THIS POINT PLEASE

What sign?"

'Ugh???'

I just couldn't believe the audacity of the man. I would like to have said,

"You know. The sign you virtually had to climb over to get to this kennel block."

But of course, I thought better of it.

The customer is always right.

The sign in question was standing at shoulder height fixed to a four-inch square oak stake. Even we had to walk around it to get to the kennel block door that was another ten yards further along.

How on earth could he have missed it?

It was impossible, so he had to be lying.

I struggled to be polite as I explained for security reasons, that we did not allow customers to just wander around our premises without being accompanied by a member of staff. He seemed to fully understand, and as a bonus, he decided to book his two dogs in the kennels for a two-week stay. On his illicit wanderings, he was very impressed with what he saw, so it does pay to bite your tongue sometimes and laugh all the way to the bank.

SIGN 15

You should be able to work this one out for yourself.

Sign 15 was fixed to the main door of kennel block two where our gentleman friend had wandered in.

NO ADMITTANCE STRICTLY STAFF ONLY

Initially, I thought about putting up a sign…

OPEN THIS DOOR AND YOU WILL BE SHOT!

Instead, I thought, be sensible here Geoff lad...

That finally seemed to sink in, because we never again had any more strangers walking around the kennels unattended.

Down to the cattery for the next few signs and we won't worry about keeping count, the numbers just kept rapidly increasing every week.

There was a simple sign...

CATTERY

I think most people could work out what that one meant!

On the outside door of the cattery...

PLEASE DO NOT OPEN THIS DOOR UNLESS ACCOMPANIED BY A MEMBER OF STAFF

That was yet another sign that was occasionally totally ignored by our curious customers.

One afternoon, we came across a small child wandering around inside the cattery. His mother had let him in because he liked stroking and playing with the nice cats.

What a nice mummy!

How they had got down to the cattery unaccompanied in the first place, was beyond belief.

Fortunately, the child couldn't get into the cat runs, we had triple spring-loaded safety doors. But he was able to touch them through the mesh doors.

If he had managed to let any out, we could have been looking for cats for weeks. His mother obviously had not seen the danger she had put her son in, and more importantly our cats.

I politely asked,

"Didn't you see the sign on the door?"

Her reply amazed me,

"I am sorry. My son just loves cats and I knew none could escape, especially with me standing here guarding the door."

In my usual polite manner, although I really could have throttled her at the time. I am not a violent person really.

I advised,

"Some of these cats can be quite aggressive and could have seriously injured your son. In fact, we have one or two in here at the moment that behave more like tigers than pet cats! Sometimes, even I am nervous of them."

After my explanation, I think the little boy's mother fully understood the danger she had put her son in and of course the lovely placid pussycats.

PLACID PUSSYCATS!!!

I have met a few cats that could have ripped her little boy's arm off!

Also, if her son had let more than one cat out there could have been cat fights and serious injuries to our feline guests. And that's not counting the chaos and mix-ups that could have happened. Also, if any cats had escaped, I hate to imagine what the cat owner's reactions would have been. Plus, who would have to tell the owners that their cats had escaped?

The child's mum eventually appreciated how she would have felt if we had lost her own cat while it was staying with us. The good news was she booked her cat in for a two-week stay.

Phew! Did we get through some traumas, or what?

My next move was to put a padlock on the outside cattery door which we kept locked when there were no members of staff in there.

I even had a sign....

COTTAGE ONLY
NO CATTERY & KENNEL BUSINESS

But we still had people knocking on our front door.

They might have said,

"Where do you want me to put my cat or dog?"

I certainly could have answered that question!!!

It was almost like my signs were trying to push the sea back with a broom. All we wanted was a bit of peace, quiet and privacy.

This is a common one...

PLEASE KEEP OFF THE GRASS

I wonder if that sign would have made any difference to the crazy Chinese Mini driver rallying on my grass.

This was the most important sign...

DANGER LOOK LEFT

I erected that sign at the very end of our driveway where it joined the busy main A41 highway. With the A41 being a long fast straight, cars were overtaking more often than not. So, when a car leaving our premises was pulling out and intending to turn left, the driver could look to the right and sometimes forget to look left without realising that cars could be overtaking from that direction. In other words, the driver's left-hand side. For readers living in the States, it would be the opposite way around.

Our sign was there to remind and warn drivers to look left as well as right. I am sure this sign saved many accidents and possibly even lives. It certainly made many people more aware of the danger.

Well, that is of course if they read it!

At least the marauding college students had the good sense not to try and nick that one.

Over the years, we only had one automobile accident, which happened to be caused by one of our customers pulling out of our drive. Fortunately, there were only minor injuries, but unfortunately, some serious damage to three vehicles.

By now you must now be getting the picture that my signs were maybe a little bit necessary. I think most people did read what they stated, but some totally ignored them or didn't even see them. It was a good job their lives didn't depend on our signs. Well, when I think about the one at the bottom of our drive, that one probably did. Not to mention other signs that could have stopped people from getting ripped to bits by big dangerous dogs or seemingly placid cats!

All of our signs were in large bold print for all to see, even if people needed reading glasses. I must say one thing about all our signs, we certainly had many a laugh over them.

I do have to add it was only a very small minority of customers this chapter referred to, but the ones that it does refer to generally gave us lots of amusement.

CHAPTER 16

The Signwriter

An embarrassing, but classic story.

I contacted Adrian, the signwriter, through Yellow Pages. It turned out that his business was new like ours. I visited Adrian's premises quite often and was amazed by how intricate the making of a sign was.

We quickly developed a good relationship and noticed each other's business grow quite rapidly. We became very good friends with Adrian and his wife Melanie and took skiing holidays together. Kathy has the honour of being godmother to their daughter Hannah.

All the signs I purchased most certainly helped Adrian to establish his new sign-writing business. I am sure I must have been one of his best customers.

This was a regular unsurprising start to one of our many phone conversations,

"Hi, Geoff, what new sign have you come up with today?"

You could say I couldn't get enough of those signs and customers did comment I had become obsessed with them.

Adrian, with his sharp wit, suggested there might be a phobia called 'sign-nar-ritus'!

Well, if there is. I certainly had it bad!

Adrian and Melanie had a cute little Yorkshire Terrier called Simon. Frequently, they took short holidays, and of course, Simon always boarded with us. When he arrived along with him came numerous toys. One of his favourite toys was a little red plastic Wellington boot. Simon used to carry it in his mouth and it squeaked when he squeezed it. He also had a small football. He would play with you for ages, hitting the ball back to you with the little red boot in his mouth, using it almost like a golf club. Amazing! He could even do headers. What a little character he was, as were many of the other boarders.

Simon plays a crucial part in the story that is soon to follow. For sure, one of the most embarrassing moments in my life!

Back to Adrian, I thought if I gave him a good boarding price for Simon, he would give me a good price for the signs.

I am sure you will know the saying, 'I'll scratch your back if you scratch mine'.

I found this statement to be true in many aspects of running our business.

Also, Adrian's brother boarded his dog with us. Who recommended him? Well, of course, it was Adrian.

Adrian and Melanie moved house quite often. No, they were not Gypsies. I think they were just obsessed with moving. Adrian loved decorating, and as soon as he had refurbished their latest house, it was sold very quickly, and they would move into their next new project, which was always bigger and of course, more valuable.

Adrian and Melanie often came to dinner at our cottage and even helped with the evening's dog walking session. We in return, were invited to their new homes. Our bonus was, we did not have to walk any dogs. Not even little Simon!

Here comes my super embarrassing story involving Simon…

We had a phone call from Adrian and Melanie inviting us for dinner at their latest house, or should I say project. Previously, we had seen the house a few months before, shortly after they purchased it. Before they bought it, the interior of the house and gardens were quite run down. It had been owned by an old lady who had not been able to look after it properly.

The house was situated in a typical beautiful English village called Ashley which is near Market Drayton in Shropshire. In that area, all the houses were very valuable and we knew it was going to be the best house they had owned so far. And hopefully, the most profitable. They were really excited for us to see the finished project and we felt highly honored because we knew we were going to be their very first visitors.

As we left our cottage, it was a cold, wet, windy winter's night and the rain was rattling the windscreen of my 4 x 4 with deafening force. Normally, Kathy opened and closed our five-bar gate, but because she had spent ages drying her long blonde hair, she didn't want it getting wet and blown about.

So, this is where Kathy's hero Geoff comes in.

BIG, BIG MISTAKE!

I slid out of the vehicle braving the screaming wind and bullets of rain, clutching and hanging on to a small black umbrella that almost turned inside-out with the force of the wind. Using one hand I dragged open the stubborn heavy wind-resisting five-bar gate, clambered back in my vehicle, drove through, slid back out holding my friend the umbrella, pulled the gate shut aided by the wind, locked the padlock, clambered back in, and finally, seriously bedraggled, set off down our winding drive…

'WHEW!!!'

What we men do for our loved ones.

We arrived at Adrian and Melanie's twenty minutes later and as we drove into their driveway, several security lights came on.

Kathy said,

Wow! Very posh.

The front door opened to reveal the excited couple beckoning us to come in. It was still blowing a 'Hooley'. The rain was lashing down more than ever.and we took a desperate dive into their porch.

We hurriedly exchanged hugs and greetings at the front door.

Thoughtfully, Kathy asked the question,

"Melanie, do you want us to take our shoes off?"

"No, just give them a good wipe on the doormat."

After meticulously wiping our shoes, we were shown into their new kitchen.

In an instant, Kathy took everything in as ladies tend to do when they walk into a new kitchen.

With a smile on her face, she said,

"Wow, this is absolutely fabulous!"

I could see Kathy was envious, she looked at me and I knew exactly what she was thinking.

"This is fantastic, Geoff. It is a lot better than ours. It has everything I could wish for."

Hey, I told you I knew what she was thinking.

We were asked what we would like to drink and shown into their lounge with its beautiful beige, almost white, plush soft carpet. It was so thick and deep.

It just had to be expensive!

After a few minutes of chatting, they left us sitting on a new cream leather settee in front of a romantic blazing fire. We were enjoying our drinks and taking in the ambience as they prepared the meal in the new kitchen. Wow, the fire was so comforting on that cold winter night, we were so shattered from a hard day's work, it would have been very easy to doze off. But we made sure we stayed politely awake as we looked around the room admiring Adrian's wallpaper. We thought how nice the colour scheme was with the pale shades complimenting each other.

Adrian was making me feel quite guilty helping Melanie in the kitchen.

Defensively I said,

"What a good husband Adrian is."

Kathy sighed and gave me a knowing look.

"Yes, I know your domain is outside with a chainsaw or lawn mower and you do your best to help me where you can in the kitchen, but it is just not your scene!"

I must say I felt a lot less guilty after her flattering comments.

We were chit-chatting generally when Kathy made a key statement,

"You know something, Adrian and Melanie are going to need to be extra careful with this carpet. It will show the slightest of marks, especially with them having Simon."

The words had barely left Kathy's mouth when I spotted...

THEM!!!

Brown marks were leading from the door, directly to where we were sitting. Or should I say to where I was sitting? The marks were a little difficult to see because the lights were dimmed.

'Kathy's right as always. This carpet is definitely the wrong colour. They're going to have real trouble keeping this clean and it looks to me like they have problems here already.'

I studied the light brown marks intensely. They were about two inches across and mark, after mark, after mark, getting darker the nearer they got to where I was sitting. They certainly had a problem all right.

And the problem led straight to me!

I knew the brown marks had nothing to do with

me because I had more than meticulously wiped my feet, observed closely by Kathy.

'Perhaps Simon made the marks before we arrived.'

I had another sip of my drink thinking the marks didn't look that fresh anyway. What a shame somebody, or something, meaning Simon, had already spoilt their beautiful new carpet. I glanced down at Kathy's shoes they looked spotless. I looked down at mine, they looked spotless. It certainly was not us that had made the horrible stains on their pale carpet. They obviously hadn't been able to get the stains out. If it had been a guilty person, what kind of moron would do something so disrespectful to a beautiful new carpet!

'I bet whoever they are, they haven't owned up to this dastardly deed.'

Drowsily I said,

"Kathy, what on earth are they doing in the kitchen? They've been in there for ages. Hey, by the way, have you noticed those marks on the carpet?"

"What marks?"

I pointed,

“Those marks over there, coming from the door.”

I had another refreshing sip from my drink.

Kathy looked at the marks in horror and said,

“It must be us!”

“No way! They’re nothing to do with us. Anyway, they’re not even fresh.”

I took another sip from my glass of superb red wine.

Kathy took off her shoes and examined the soles underneath.

“Geoff, my shoes are clean! Check yours.”

That sounded like an order straight from the top!

“I told you before, mine are clean and the stains on the carpet are old.”

Kathy gave that look that only your wife can give you.

"Will you please do as I ask? And take them off?"

'I'm tempted to give a sergeant major's salute.'

I took my right shoe off.

I waved it at her.

"Look! It's clean. I told you so."

I knew I wasn't the cause of the stains, so I never bothered taking off my left shoe. Relaxing, I glanced down at it and moved my ankle to turn the shoe onto its side.

'OH NO!!!'

My heart skipped a beat!

I stared down in horror...

Because staring right back up at me was...

The biggest piece of brown dog turd that was possible to implant directly in the middle of my instep.

'ARGHHH!!!'

The horrible thing must have weighed at least two ounces.

Oh no!

Why hadn’t I felt it?

Why hadn’t I smelt it?

Why hadn’t it come off when I wiped my feet?

And why hadn’t I seen it?

Oh why, oh why, oh why?

The grotesque piece of dog turd was artistically curled up on the right side of my shoe and looked like a horn. It was so sculptured it could have adorned a Viking's helmet!

A cobbler couldn't have made a more precise job!

It was a work of art.

And it stared back up at me triumphantly.

I stared back in horror…

‘ARRRRRRGHHHHH!!!’

I shrieked under my breath, not wanting to alert our hosts, who very soon could become our enemies.

Kathy looked at my shocked red face and said,

"WHAT'S WRONG?"

"Shh! Look at my shoe."

She looked at my shoe and her face filled with horror and disgust.

"Oh no Geoff!"

"Perhaps they won't notice."

"Of course, they will notice."

"What am I going to do?"

"You'll have to tell them!"

"I'm not telling them. You tell them!'

"No! It's on your shoe. You tell them. This is all because you haven't bothered to wipe your shoes properly!"

"Of course, I did. You saw me. You even watched me. How was I to know I had a massive piece of dog turd stuck beneath the instep of my shoe?"

"You should have checked your shoes better!"

"Why didn't we smell it in the car? It's too big to belong to their Yorkshire Terrier. I must have picked it up from our gate when I opened and closed it. You should have done the gate. You always open and close it. Just because you were frightened of getting your hair messed up. It's not fair. It should be on your shoe, not on mine!"

My temper and embarrassment were rising by the second.

"I'll kill those girls at the kennels tomorrow morning. They must have walked the long-haired dogs down the drive because it was so muddy in the wood today. If I have told them once, I've told them a thousand times to clear up any dog crap lying down that drive. Just wait until tomorrow. I'll give them a rollicking they will never forget."

Kathy interrupted my flow of heightening anticipation for the next morning's rollicking or even better...Strangling's!

“Never mind what you’ll do tomorrow. What are you going to do tonight? What are you going to say to Adrian and Melanie?”

“Oh, I don’t know. Do you think it will come off the carpet?”

“Probably… But what are you going to say to them?”

‘It’s all right for Miss Perfect innocently sitting there. It’s not on her shoe, is it? It’s on my shoe!’

Then the inevitable happened, Melanie shouted,

“Are you all right in there? We’ll be with you in a second.”

‘No, we are not!’

I was getting really worried about my impending embarrassment.

I whispered,

“Kathy, what am I going to say?”

“Knowing you I am sure you will find the right words.”

'A fat lot of help that is!'

The next minute Melanie walked through the door with a nice big beaming smile on her face.

Holding her drink, she looked at me with a concerned look on her face and said,

"Geoff, are you okay? You look a little red in the face?"

'Of course, I'm red in the face.'

'I'm red in the face with embarrassment!'

'I'm red in the face because I have messed up your brand new very expensive beautiful carpet.'

'I'm red in the face because I've spread dog crap all over your new carpet and you haven't even noticed.'

'And I've got to own up to all this crap, haven't I!'

I pulled myself together and politely stammered out,

"How long will Adrian be? I've got something to tell you both."

I certainly wasn't going to own up to my mess by telling Melanie first and then having to go through the same nightmare scenario again with Adrian. I thought it would be best to tell them together and get it all over and done with in one go.

Talk about, 'Killing two birds with one stone'!

I knew I had to tell them as soon as possible, before I lost my nerve and blamed their Yorkie, Simon.

What a devious idea that would be!

'My next drink is definitely going to be brandy.'

'That's if I live long enough to take another drink!'

Adrian came into the lounge, proudly beaming from ear to ear with a drink in his hand.

I looked up at him.

'I'll soon wipe that smile off your face mate when I tell you the good news about your once beautiful new carpet!'

"So, what do you think of our new house then?

Do you like how we decorated it?

And what about the new colour scheme?"

He was so proud he could hardly wait for us to answer the previous question before he asked the next.

And then he said the dreaded words,

"Don't you think it goes well with the carpet?"

'ARGHHH!!!'

Carpet! Carpet!

I couldn't believe what I was hearing. My hands had started to shake and I almost spilt my wine over my smart white jeans. I even had beads of sweat forming on my forehead.

'This is a nightmare. What are you going to think of my new colour scheme on your carpet? Oh no someone please help me. Beam me up, Scotty. Get me out of here right now!'

Bravely, I composed myself for the oncoming holocaust. I put my hand to my mouth and gave a slight cough and then grovelled,

"I'm so terribly, terribly sorry. There is something I need to own up to."

Slowly but surely, their smiles started to evaporate as I nervously explained the shocking news. I hit them with the full story of how I must have acquired the larger-than-life Vikings helmet dog turd. And what I was going to do to the girls in the morning.

Surprisingly, they didn't throw up or throw me out. They took my devastating news exceptionally well. They could see how terribly embarrassed I was and were so understanding. They even gave me a glass of their best brandy to calm my frayed nerves.

Now, that is what you call good friends!

It was the first and last time I will ever be invited to anyone's house and spend over half an hour on my hands and knees wearing my best clothes, cleaning up dog crap from a brand-new carpet.

In fact, any carpet at all.

And to crap it all, (sorry a slip of the tongue) I mean to cap it all, their little Yorkshire Terrier Simon had already been banned from going into their newly carpeted lounge. I had even been deviously thinking how I could have blamed him for the dastardly deed. The poor little dog would have taken at least a week of crapping to produce a turd the size of the monster that had attached itself under the instep of my shoe.

The good news is, it was a happy ending because the carpet was cleaned up as good as new, with no trace of the crappy marks to be seen at all.

Hey, hang on a minute it was new.

So, no harm done. We enjoyed a lovely evening with the proud couple in their beautiful new home along with a few more clinks of glasses.

And I made doubly sure that I purchased another sign from Adrian within the week, just to make sure I was really back in his good books.

A few years after I wrote this story, Adrian and Melanie came to visit us in Spain and the amazing thing is, they couldn't even remember my extremely embarrassing incident. Kathy and I couldn't believe they had forgotten something that we thought was so important, or to put it mildly, to us a major catastrophe.

Especially for me!

Surely, both of us didn't dream the same nightmare?

I can tell you over the years Kathy and I, with lots of different friends, have had some laughs over that little incident.

CHAPTER 17

Screams in the Bedroom

A knight in shining armour.

This is yet another animal story, in fact, two stories, but slightly different, because it has nothing at all to do with cats or dogs, perhaps that makes a welcome change.

These events took place when Ann, Kathy's sister was staying with us.

One night, after the three of us had completed a successful day's work and enjoyed a lovely meal with a nice bottle of wine, with of course the usual conversation of 'Dinner Talk', which you will understand if you read Book III in this series.

Kathy, Ann and I were sitting in front of our log fire relaxing and watching the TV. We were getting sleepy-eyed, so we decided to retire to bed, leaving Ann downstairs in the lounge. Ann usually stayed up quite late and even these days that habit hasn't changed. It would be an understatement to say she was a bit of a 'Night Owl'. Ann, by the way, loves owls and there were plenty of them inhabiting the area where we lived. There were tawny owls, little owls and we were lucky enough to have the beautiful rare barn owls as well.

Anyway, that's enough of owls!

Ann had a big, big phobia and still has to this very day, which this first story will soon reveal and I reiterate it is nothing to do with owls. I had no idea what time it was on that memorable night. Kathy and I were in a deep sleep when an ear-piercing high-pitched scream made us sit bolt upright in bed.

I said,

"Kathy! What on earth was that?

Well, I didn't have to wait very long, before another ear-piercing scream erupted from somewhere in our cottage.

It was human and it could only have belonged to one person.

ANN!

Quickly I jumped into my jeans and raced along to Ann's bedroom which was at the far end of the cottage. By then, the hysterical screaming was continuous and obviously coming from within

Ann’s bedroom.

Well, Geoff the hero, had no choice but to burst through Ann's bedroom door and maybe, just maybe, save her life.

‘What on earth am I going to find when I burst through this door!’

I burst through...

The sight that greeted me was Ann in her night attire perched perilously on the top of her bedhead with tears flooding down her cheeks. She couldn’t have put more distance between her and the bedroom floor if she tried.

I looked around the bedroom and I couldn’t see anything obvious that could have created Ann's incredibly distressed condition.

I suppose the good news was, at least there were only two of us in her bedroom that were human!

I looked at her curiously and said,

“Whatever is wrong with you?”

Ann pointed her finger at the floor...

She shrieked hysterically,

"THERE! THERE! THERE!"

"What are you shouting at? I can't see anything. Have you been dreaming?"

"No, I haven't been dreaming. There's a great big frog in my magazine."

Now you know exactly what Ann's terrifying phobia is...

FROGS AND TOADS!

"Why on earth are you reading magazines with pictures of frogs and toads in at this time of the night? You know they frighten you to death."

In her exasperation, she hysterically screamed out,

"IT'S NOT A PICTURE YOU FOOL!"

"IT'S ALIVE!"

Well, I didn't blame Ann for panicking. Because what I eventually found under her bed innocently looking back at me was not a frog, but a half-grown toad.

You might be thinking, how on earth can a half-grown toad, that can't jump like frogs, end up on the upstairs floor of our cottage in Ann's bedroom?

Nothing to do with me. For sure! I can play some pranks, but not the sort that is likely to give someone a heart attack.

No, this poor little toad had unbelievingly crept into Ann's magazine, which had coincidentally been lying on the hall floor by the front door. The door must have been left ajar for a short period of time during that autumn evening.

So, Mr Toad must have crept in and hidden between the pages.

Incredibly, poor Ann had carried the hapless little toad up into her bedroom. Ann was single at that time and I am sure she would not have minded if Mr Toad had turned into a handsome Prince. I am sure you must have heard or read about the Brothers Grimm story. It is about a Princess, a Toad and a handsome Prince. As we all know, it is kissing the toad that makes it turn into a handsome Prince. So for sure, Ann was never going to meet her Prince that night, or any night, because as sure as can be, she would never kiss a toad in a million years.

Or even for a million pounds!

Anyway, I gently picked up Ann's little friend, Mr Toad, not the handsome Prince and transported him down the stairs to release him onto our front lawn, where he will have enjoyed feeding on the many earthworms that inhabited there.

So, that is the toad problem sorted out.

Now it is Ann's turn.

We soon sorted her out with a glass of brandy to calm her nerves. In fact, all three of us ended up with a glass.

Hey, any excuse will do!

Well, it did help us sleep after our sudden shock of being woken up by Ann's ear-piercing high-pitched screams.

Is that a Toad or a Prince?

Here is another story featuring Ann...

We had another hysterical screaming session coming from Ann that was also late at night. A story similar to the previous one. But, this one was with an entirely different animal...

Not one that inhabited the ground...

But one that inhabited...

The sky!

So with more hysterical screams from the bedroom and Geoff playing the hero yet again, I burst into Ann's bedroom to rescue her from…

What was I going to find this time?

Well, guess what I found?

Flying around her bedroom…

It was not a bird…

It was not a plane…

And it was not Batman either…

It was a little bat!

A tiny pipistrelle to be precise.

And boy, did it take some catching that night!

The first thing I did, was to get the hysterical screaming sister out of her bedroom.

The next thing I did was to fetch one of my fishing accessories...

A landing net.

I can't tell you how much I enjoy swishing a landing net around in the early hours of the morning.

The tiny bat was very, very quick and elusive. Boy, did it take some time to catch it?

When I finally caught the tiny creature, I released it unharmed into the night sky to rejoin the rest of its mates flitting around hunting moths by using their amazing sonar.

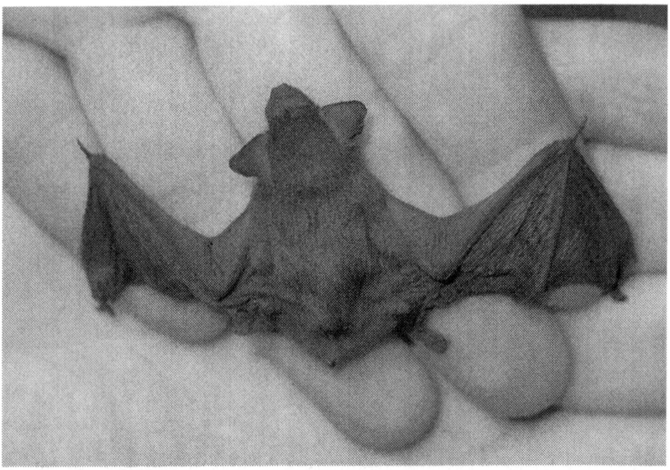

A diminutive pipistrelle bat. How small is that?

I concluded that the tiny bat must have squeezed

through the loft hatch, which was unfortunate for poor Ann because it was situated in the ceiling of her room, right above the head of the bed.

We classed ourselves as being lucky, but some people might say unlucky because it turned out that we had a very large bat colony in our attic. We knew there was a lot up there because at night when we had our front security light on, hundreds of bats were criss-crossing and zooming around at speed, hunting and feeding on moths from the woodland. With there being so many, it was amazing that they didn't crash into each other, but of course, they wouldn't because they were using sonar that is designed to hunt the moths and avoid collisions.

A year after Ann's traumatic incident, I phoned a person at the Nature Conservancy who was very keen to visit our premises to observe the bats. It was late summer when a young female professor turned up in the evening. Her visit had been arranged by phone. She was blonde wearing her hair up and sporting wire-rim glasses, as most professors always seem to do. She was an expert on bats and had come to take a bat count.

At dusk, the adult female bats were leaving their offspring in the nursery to hunt moths in the surrounding woodland and would be out all night until they returned at dawn.

The four of us, meaning the professor, Ann, Kathy and I, stood outside with our backs to the walls at various points of our cottage. Each of us had a counter in our hand which we pressed with a clicking sound every time a bat left the nursery in our attic.

Amazingly, the total of pipistrelle bats came to over two thousand six hundred.

WOW!

The professor informed us that we had the second-largest colony in the UK.

Can you believe that?

After that astounding discovery, the professor was very keen to come back again on a morning, to observe the resting/sleeping bats in our attic. Eventually, when she did come back, with me being very interested in anything to do with nature, we went up into the attic together to observe the amazing phenomenon.

I had insulated the loft many years before and the insulation between the joists comprised of yellow fibreglass cladding. On top of it, I had laid strips of white-coloured polystyrene, which had become very faded.

Under the professor's guidance, I slowly and very gently raised one of the polystyrene sheets.

We looked underneath and in unison, both jerked back…

What we observed...

Was...

UNBELIEVABLE!!!

It was absolutely seething with bats!

HUNDREDS AND HUNDREDS OF THEM!!!

Bat heads and wings were joined up in one writhing mass!

Imagine, getting that lot in your hair girls!

I am sure our Ann would have been in one heck of a panic if that lot had been flitting around her bedroom!

CHAPTER 18

Once in a Lifetime

This final story is about the Woodcock Man.

Meaning me!

This fantastic mind-blowing experience of mine was published in Birdwatching Magazine, UK and USA in 2022. For those of you that are interested in nature, I think you will enjoy it.

This is an amazing once-in-a-lifetime story about the mysterious woodland bird, the woodcock. This amazing occurrence took place well before we built the pet hotel/cattery & kennels. This unique experience happened when I was the last in the line of gamekeepers working from our cottage, Keepers Cottage.

My love of birds began very early in life. By the age of ten, I knew virtually every bird and egg in the British Observers Book series.

To experience the following story, that was never believed by experts, puts me amongst a mere handful of blessed people on the planet.

Unlike the Scottish Loch Ness Monster, Nessie.

My story is true!

The one hundred acres of mixed woodland were situated within yards of the picturesque gamekeeper's cottage. The wood consisted of oak, mountain ash, silver birch and Scots pine. A perfect habitat for the elusive ground-nesting wader, the woodcock (scolapax rusticola). Also, a perfect habitat for my wife Kathy and my cute Springer Spaniel, Sally.

Woodcock, also known as the snipe of the woods, were quite common in the 80s and we loved to watch the males throughout the spring and summer performing their roding flights (breeding display) at dusk. Woodcocks are rarely seen by humans because they spend most of their time on the ground and protect themselves by sitting perfectly still allowing their camouflage to render them virtually invisible. It was lucky for us that the woodcock exhibits one of the most conspicuous breeding displays in the avian world. Male woodcock, attract females (as many as four) and always keep to the same flight pattern. They generally fly at treetop height on their territorial circuit.

From our garden every evening at exactly the same time Kathy and I, not forgetting Sally, watched an approaching male, which in all probability would be the same bird from the evening before. As the male woodcock passed directly above us, he emitted base-sounding grunts or croaks and haunting high-pitched whistles. I loved the experience of observing these fascinating birds and it was not long before I became obsessed with the mysterious woodcock.

One very memorable day, I was very lucky to find a nest, or should I say, my Springer Sally did.

The nest was quite close to a ride (pathway) cut through part of the one-hundred-acre woodland that had been replanted with Scots pine. The young trees had rapidly achieved a height of twenty feet or so. Sally was walking obediently by my side. Suddenly, she froze, lifted her left paw, and pointed directly at something on the ground with her shiny black nose. Standing absolutely still, resting my left hand on my trusty V-shaped hazel thumb stick, I could see nothing. I waited a good half minute…

Nothing moved…

Including Sally.

With mounting curiosity and anticipation, I motioned to Sally by showing her the palm of my hand to sit and stay. I took great care where I put my feet as I walked towards Sally's nose-pointed area no more than eight feet away.

Suddenly, right in front of me, with a flutter and whir of wings, a woodcock exploded from a tiny mound of dead pine needles and zigzagged away through the closely planted conifers. I kept my eyes rooted to the spot that she had vacated as I carefully closed in…

To my joy, lying in a hollow amongst the pine

needles were four extremely well-camouflaged brown, grey and orange blotchy eggs. For a couple of minutes, I took in the memorable scene photographed forever by my brain. I planned to come back to check the progress of the eggs, so with the nest being so incredibly camouflaged, I reached into my trouser pocket and produced my red Swiss Army penknife. Using the largest blade, I made a small mark on the trunk of the nearest tree to the right of the woodcock's nest. With the mark complete, I backed off, making sure that I had left no trail for a predator or human eyes to notice.

A clutch of well-camouflaged woodcock eggs on the woodland floor

Three days later, I returned to my secretly

marked pine tree by the nest to ensure that my disturbance had not forced the female woodcock to forsake her eggs. I stood with Sally sitting at heel on the edge of the ride and stared intensely for a good minute at the covering of pine needles scattered on the ground. Finally, I breathed a sigh of relief, because there looming in my vision was the large bright eye of the woodcock giving the highly camouflaged bird's game away. Feeling completely satisfied, I smiled at her, turned and walked away.

A well-camouflaged woodcock sitting on a nest on the woodland floor. Do you notice the bright eye?

A week later, I returned, and to my joy, I found that all four eggs had hatched successfully. I knew that within a very short time, the hatchlings would have scurried away led by their mother to safety.

This is where my woodcock story gets even better…

I am sure envied by many, at 7 am every morning, Sally and I had the habit of taking the same walk along an old cart track that entered the oak part of the wood. The oaks were less than a stone's throw away from our snail-patterned (pointed cement) mauve sandstone cottage. It was a sunny June morning without a single cloud to interrupt a crystal-clear cobalt sky. Sally and I had only walked thirty yards or so when I was startled as a medium-sized brown shape flashed low over us from behind…

It was a woodcock.

Instantly, I realised there was something very unusual in the way it was flying. In fact, it appeared to be struggling. To my astonishment, it was plain to see that the woodcock had its tail fanned out with four legs protruding from within. In a thousandth of a second, I knew exactly what that meant…

This female woodcock was carrying young!

And only a handful of people on the planet had

ever witnessed it!!!

Instantly, I was incredibly excited and gave chase. And boy, I could run in those days. With a surprised and excited Sally running by my side, I ran like crazy and leapt over bracken and briars as I kept my eye on the departing female woodcock.

To my relief, she flopped down about twenty yards in front of us, vanishing in the three-foot-high bright green bracken. Keeping my eyes peeled on the exact spot where she had landed and with Sally staying close, probably wondering what on earth was going on, quickly but carefully, I pushed my way through the bracken. When I arrived at the spot of the woodcock's disappearance, I gently parted the bracken aside with my hands. I searched for a couple of minutes but to no avail…

No woodcock.

To my amazement, I was startled yet again by a woodcock swooping from above that appeared to come from nowhere. It divebombed quite close to my head. I looked on in wonderment as her powerful wings beat a hasty zigzag retreat between the multitude of oak branches.

Unfortunately, Sally with her keen nose and I never found the youngster on the leaf-covered woodland floor. I assumed that it had been ushered away by the mother to a safe spot before she came back to divebomb me, hoping to decoy my attention away from her offspring.

I was stunned. I had proved to myself that woodcock do carry their young and I had the incredible privilege to witness it.

Even if I had a camera with me on that crystal clear sunny June day, with the spectacular event happening so quickly, I was never in a position to film it.

To this day, the elusive woodcock has never been filmed carrying young. I was incredibly fortunate to witness that mysterious woodcock phenomenon. Especially at that time when most ornithologists' bodies believed that it was an 'Old Wives Tale'.

Nowadays, ornithologist experts accept stories like mine.

The elusive woodcock does carry their young.

So, for me, how lucky is that?

What a truly unforgettable vivid memory.

Now that you have gained some remarkable knowledge about the elusive woodcock.

Maybe, you will want to gain some more knowledge from the next book in this series, especially if you are crazy enough to want to open a pet hotel of your own!

ACKNOWLEDGEMENT

To my incredible wife Kathy, who has had the patience of a saint to work with me over the years that it has taken me to publish this book. She painstakingly typed my awful long hand and helped to revamp it hundreds of times into this wonderful humorous collection of stories.

My sincere thanks to Mick, who has drawn the outstanding detailed caricatures giving the book its very own unique personality.

I would like to thank all my family, friends, and customers. And of course, not forgetting the main characters, the cats and dogs who created the stories.

A special thanks to my managers, Clare, Debbie, Kick, Pat and Erica.

And to all my girls, Tracey, Haley, Jenny, Gill, Hannah, Caroline, Charlotte, Amy and any other staff that I might have inadvertently left out.

Although all the stories are based on true facts, some names have been changed to protect identities.

AUTHOR BIO

Geoff was born in Newport, a small historic market town in the county of Shropshire, England. Here, he was involved in various businesses. His diversified career ranged from, shopkeeper, restauranter, sales rep, gamekeeper, builder. And finally, the pet hotel that inspired Geoff's very funny autobiographical stories in this three-book series.

The pet hotel known as Chetwynd Firs, is still situated in an idyllic spot north of Newport, off the A41 highway. Newport is very close to the Staffordshire border; therefore, the business served those two counties, plus Cheshire and a large part of the Midlands.

Geoff and Kathy live in Thailand with three cats, Drambuie, Sambuca and Tia Maria.

Printed in Great Britain
by Amazon

36439838R00227